OUTRAGEOUS
FORTUNE

OUTRAGEOUS FORTUNE

Gloomy Reflections on Luck and Life

WILLIAM IAN MILLER

OXFORD
UNIVERSITY PRESS

OXFORD
UNIVERSITY PRESS

Oxford University Press is a department of the University of Oxford. It furthers
the University's objective of excellence in research, scholarship, and education
by publishing worldwide. Oxford is a registered trade mark of Oxford University
Press in the UK and certain other countries.

Published in the United States of America by Oxford University Press
198 Madison Avenue, New York, NY 10016, United States of America.

Library of Congress Cataloging-in-Publication Data
Names: Miller, William Ian, 1946– author.
Title: Outrageous fortune : gloomy reflections on luck and life / William Ian Miller.
Description: New York : Oxford University Press, 2021. |
Includes bibliographical references and index.
Identifiers: LCCN 2020023114 (print) | LCCN 2020023115 (ebook) |
ISBN 9780197530689 (hardback) | ISBN 9780197530702 (epub)
Subjects: LCSH: Fortune.
Classification: LCC BD595 .M55 2021 (print) | LCC BD595 (ebook) |
DDC 128—dc23
LC record available at https://lccn.loc.gov/2020023114
LC ebook record available at https://lccn.loc.gov/2020023115

1 3 5 7 9 8 6 4 2

Printed by Sheridan Books, Inc., United States of America

In memory of Donald C. Koehler (d. June 7, 2019), teacher and father-in-law

"I am not well . . . "
—Shylock

CONTENTS

ACKNOWLEDGMENTS

———◆———

I wish to thank Annalise Acorn, Jordan Corrente Beck, Dan Crane, John Crigler, Don Herzog, John Hudson, and Mark West for reading and commenting on various drafts. And thanks for specific inputs to Andrew Cecchinato, Rich Friedman, Abigail Hartman, Ingrid Hedström, and Nina Mendelson. Thanks too to Anna Becker who designed the cover and to my editor at Oxford University Press, Cynthia Read, who, along with other sage advice, suggested the title, wisely saving me the humiliation of my initial offerings: *Naying from Gulliver's Stable* (yes, Naying), or *Liver of Blaspheming Jew*. Even I knew, I think, that neither of these would end up the title.

About a third of chapter 1 appeared as "May You Have My Luck," *The Chronicle Review, The Chronicle of Higher Education*, February 6, 2015. Chapter 4—"Vile Jelly"—is an expanded and revised version of "Epilogue: Do I Disgust You? (Or Rather, You Me?) mes frères, mes sœurs, mes semblables?" in *Le Dégoût: Histoire, langage, esthétique et politique*, edited by Michel Delville, Andrew Norris, and Viktoria von Hoffmann (Presses Universitaires de Liège, 2015), 149–61. And a version of chapter 5 appeared as "The Messenger," in *Frieden stiften: Vermittlung und Konfliktslösung vom Mittelalter bis heute*, edited by Gerd Althoff (Darmstadt: WBG, 2011), 19–36.

Ann Arbor, 2020

A Somewhat Dour Introduction

NOW THAT WE LIVE so long, retirement poses an insistent peril. Each new day eyes me with disapproval, having learned from its predecessor that I did nothing that could justify the food and drink I consumed the day before. Admonishing spirits, though I cannot see them, prove their presence in stage whispers. They do not let me, a chronic insomniac, feel as if I *accomplished* something because I actually managed five hours of sleep assisted by only one Ambien. Their whispers grow harsher, especially at bedtime, threatening revenge for the five hours I managed the night before. Not a chance in hell I will get five hours of sleep tonight, even with three Ambien, washed down by a shot of whisky.

Sure, my antidepressants can help make me feel less like I am criminally wasting the new day, reducing my sense of culpability from felony to misdemeanor. Read the newspapers (online)? Not even opioids could dull the despair they evoke. But when at seventy-four I have an exceptionally healthy mother who is ninety-eight and tests out as if she were fifty, my fear is that I might have quite a few more years to fill or kill, though hardly twenty-four of them—I have only half her genes anyway, and male mortality is higher than female at every age. Her health, a blessing to the intelligent yet innately cheerful her, threatens me, a nerve-addled pessimist, with untoward longevity, a genetic curse. Even if, as I suspect, my pessimism is in part an act, I am incapable of not performing it. It is a trait that can be attributed to my father's way of being in the world when he was in it. Not an ounce of irony could interfere with his seeing a harbinger of Nuremburg rallies in ranks of fluffy fair-weather cumulus clouds drifting slowly across the summer sky. And he was born and raised in Green Bay, Wisconsin, not even in the Baltic his parents had the fortune to flee at the beginning of the twentieth century.

I hate the phrase that now has become the obligatory riposte to my tiresome complaints about aging, its aches, debilities, and demoralizations—a phrase mostly voiced by old people but that has trickled down to people much younger: "better than the alternative," they say. If the alternative is having to accept a world in which that passes for wit, let me walk over and touch the wire. If all they mean to do is politely put a halt to my kvetching, then I guess I had it coming, but to the extent they are actually signing on to the sentiment (as most speakers over seventy are), I fear they are already in the midst of an alternative they have not fully considered. Like, say, dementia. Nor do they seem to have accounted for the likely alternative of nursing homes, a kinder kind of death camp. Or somewhat less bleakly, they have not yet thought of what it means to be objects of those twinges of resentment even an otherwise decent person might feel when old people get to board the plane first, whether they can do so under their own power or have to be wheeled on. "Better than the alternative" encapsulates the deep cowardice that seems to fund our antiheroic never-die-at-no-matter-what-the-cost way of life; otherwise, why not say as we used to: "oh stop complaining already"?[1]

I do have a soft side. Ask my dog, the cats, even the two turtles and the mouse we just saved (and caged) from one of the cats who teamed up with the dog to make the catch. An hour earlier we could hear him rummaging behind the microwave. These creatures are all sources of pleasure and reminders that beauty and good still exist in the non-human world at least, and damn if that cute field mouse, no bigger than the unshelled peanut we put in a small cage we readied for him, or one of his larger house-mice cousins, was not also the source of what I thought were the tasteless caraway or cumin seeds I was trapping on the counter with my wet index finger and eating up as I did the dishes. (While revising this two weeks after it was first drafted I checked on the mouse, who would hide under the wood shavings in his cage. He/she was dead. I was surprised at how much it got me all Hamletted up about the meaninglessness of everything.)

Nonetheless, I have had it pretty good, and still objectively have it so, and yet I complain, and find myself filled with homicidal fury at texters for whom I must step out of the way (I said that in my book *Losing It* some ten years ago, but my irritation has only increased, as has the number of inattentive self-involved texters). If one counts it as good luck to have been a tenured professor at a good school teaching and writing only about what I wanted to, then so too those texters have been very lucky at my commendable reserves of self-restraint in not applying for a conceal-carry permit. So lucky do I count myself that two of the chapters that follow will deal with the anxieties that good luck generates and the evil it portends. But to make sure I keep pressing my luck, I continue riding helmetless a 900-pound 1800cc motorcycle contraindicated for six months in deference to my recent urethroplasty.[2] I refuse to accept that the bike is in any way a symbolic prosthetic as I fear some might think it is, but it does put my arthritic knees to the test at every stoplight. And my normal cruising speeds force me to douse my now discless cervical vertebrae with a salve of medical marijuana to alleviate the ache of keeping my head up in the wind and thus my incipiently cataracted eyes on the road.

I do not wish to repeat, more than I already have and will allow myself in this and the next paragraph, the scorn I poured in *Losing It* on the prevalent (and lucrative) idiotic upbeat view of aging except to say this: I might have played up my claims of decline then in hopes of placating the gods by not taking too generous a view of my mental and physical condition. Nope, it did not work. The gods soon let me know that I had presumed on their beneficence. They turned any exaggerations of decline I might have made then—maybe they heard them as whining and there is nothing, absolutely nothing, that excuses whining—into understatements. Confidence dies as I can no longer concentrate on what I am reading without concentrating on the very process of concentration, thereby intercepting the concentration I need to direct to the task at hand. Surely you know what I mean. I in fact just wrote "you no what I mean." I have always had difficulty distinguishing homophones, one seeming as good as another and not randomly either, for I am more likely to write *right* or *rite* for *write*, *discussed* for *disgust*, than to hit on the proper one, and the spellchecker shares my disability. There was a kid a year behind me in high school who was diagnosed as schizophrenic in his junior year, or so we were told, but one of his new-found abilities was to find homophones in the strangest of places. One that stuck in my memory requires recalling the technology of dialing a telephone: said he to a friend visiting him in the locked ward: "Do your pupils dilate when you dial 8?"

For a writer the real curse is the shrinking of vocabulary. Words once readily available are playing hide and seek. The word you wanted to give your writing some elegance, or pizazz, or precision, ran off somewhere (hence my recourse to *pizazz*). When that happens in conversation, one is put to a refrain of insipidities: "Well you know what I mean, I mean, oh damn, I'm blanking on the word, oh god, this happens all the time now, what was I saying again? It will come to me." (It often doesn't, and if it does, I do not recognize it as the word or intention I had lost earlier anyway.)

Even if all this self-deprecation is overdone false modesty, do not completely discount it. There is more than an ounce of truth to it, maybe a full-fleshed pound. I have always felt each age, from mid-childhood well into my seventies, to be a kind of obstacle course in a game called Humiliation, where the desperate goal is not to be laughed at. Every day seems to offer up its version of wiping out on the ice, without the luck of it being unwitnessed. *Humiliation*. The very word is like a bell tolling me back to my first volume of essays, published in 1993, around a set of related themes indicated by its title, *Humiliation*. Here is one fairly recent example among many I could confess to.

I cannot recall the exact year this happened, sometime around 2008 or so, nor exactly who the people were before which it took place. Some who were there might challenge the details, but the main action is true, painfully true. It was a dinner following a talk I gave at All Souls College Oxford. Then came high table and I did not have the appropriate dress, the mandatory dinner jacket. No equity was available to relieve me of the rigors of that law. They rummaged about and found a coat reserved for such vulgar guests as I, but it did not fit. It would have been perfect for a man some six inches shorter, three or four inches in the sleeves alone, and eighty pounds heavier than I was. In short, I was reduced to looking like a clown. And since clothes truly do make the man, as I was about to prove, I ended up confirming the justice of my outfit with deeds to match. Maybe that jacket had a powerful will of its own, feeling no less disgraced clothing me than I felt being clothed by it. To maintain dignity would require more poise than I could muster.

The wine served soon after the prayer, with Christ in it of course, was superb, and I downed my first glass rather quickly, not to inebriate myself, but because it was so very much better than the fare I normally treat myself to. It tasted so good, and I am not much given to sipping, but rather more to 'quaffing,' the word with which the Passover Haggadah (the prayer book for the Seder) we used when I was a kid, with its immigrant instinct for exotic English words heading at breakneck speed for obsolescence, ordered the drinking of the ritually mandatory four cups of nauseatingly sweet wine: "Quaff the fourth cup of wine."

Now I must allude to Thor in a story told by Snorri Sturluson in his *Prose Edda* (early thirteenth century).[3] Thor, on a journey east to Jotunheim, the land of giants, ends up at the castle of Útgarðaloki, who puts Thor to any test Thor should choose to exhibit his skills at. Thor chooses drinking, he being the drinking champion among the gods. Útgarðaloki provides Thor with a drinking horn and Thor gulps and guzzles in grand style but finds he makes not the smallest dent in the level of the horn. Thor is mystified at his failing; a second try does no better; on the third attempt, mustering all his will, he manages to lower the level of the horn a miniscule but visible amount. Thor, defeated, gives up and hands the horn back. Útgarðaloki mocks him but in the end reveals that the horn had been connected to the sea, and when he sends Thor on his way he shows him the sandy shore he had drunk enough to carve out from the ocean.

Why is this story relevant? Because my glass of wine, no matter how much I drank, and drank, stayed at the same level. Half-beknownst to me were attentive waiters, very attentive, who kept topping up my glass. I grew more and more voluble, holding forth on whatever topic anyone chose to raise. People seemed interested in what I had to say, but God only knows what I was saying. Dinner came and went; a different wine with a new unemptiable glass connected to the sea was provided for each course, never requiring that I go through the motions of pouring myself; and then it was time to repair to another room to have a post-prandial whisky. I stood up, and lo, I stumbled forward, knocking over, spilling, and shattering several glasses of red wine onto the white tablecloth, before which I saw a group of English faces swimming.

In retrospect, I wonder if this was a test, not of my drinking capacity nor even devised as a plot designed to confirm their prejudices regarding the vulgarity and lack of gentility of Americans, and an American Jew at that, than a test of their own capacity for tact and graciousness, for no one made me feel any sillier for that disaster than I had already felt dressed in that jacket. The postprandial drinking went on, as far as I could tell, swimmingly.

I was, it seems, quite drunk but not so much so that a quick flash of shame did not hit me when I knocked over the glasses, but the malt whisky was so good I was soon at ease in complete shamelessness, until the 3 AM sickening horrors of self-evaluation took over. I should add that I was never invited back. Observing my humiliation were not just the living people there but portraits of prior fellows of All Souls looking nobly down from the walls, but with expressions of marked disapproval. Among them were my heroes, W. P. Ker,[4] the greatest reader of the sagas ever; E. E. Evans-Pritchard, the anthropologist I most admired; and David Daube, omniscient in Bible, Talmud, and Roman law. Even T. E. Lawrence managed to look down on me, though only five foot five at the max, but hung up high enough on the wall as if wearing specially stacked heels.[5] What in hell was I doing there, which was the same question my hosts were asking themselves.

The point of this tale? That one can survive a giant misstep in the game of Humiliation? That is for you to decide. It is hard for an academic to have more than one idea, if that; it is even harder not to repeat the few ideas you have had; and it is still harder not to convince yourself that you are not repeating yourself, which belief is aided by your inability to remember what you have written in the last thirty years. Sometimes the revisitation might lead to improving earlier positions and, if lucky, to coming up with a new micro-idea or some insight, which, as far as your modest researches indicate, is original. I have convinced myself that that is the case here.

Some of the chapters of this book were tested in embryonic form before live audiences in formal lectures over the last decade or so; others will be first tested on you. The book has a unity of voice, of view, and of several interlaced themes: the scarcity of good, the tinge of ominousness that accompanies good luck, the intrusiveness of the belief that our desires and wishes provoke the gods to lengthen the odds against their fulfillment. On occasion, I offer banal advice: like never count a chicken before it is hatched, for the very counting will blast the embryo. Certain topics I never seem able to avoid—getting even, competitiveness, humiliation, and disgust with human embodiment—will play their parts, spiced with particular attention to killing messengers bearing both good and bad tidings, to the decline of everything (including me), to an occasional eye-gouging, to more autobiography than might be seemly, to bitterness at the back-to-business-as-usual resurrection of Jew hating and baiting, and finally to breaking bread and bodies with Jesus at the Last Supper.

I have promised myself to keep references to my beloved Icelandic sagas to a minimum. I could not, however, keep them out entirely, since they have so permeated my soul as to make me the person I am. Somewhat remarkably, I pretty much have kept my promise (the story of Thor's drinking comes not from a saga but from an *edda*, a term known to most crossword puzzle addicts). I have not larded the book with endnotes to secondary literature unless I knowingly stole the thought cited or require it for added proof of a claim I am making. I do, however, allow myself several endnotes that I find interesting in their own right but do not quite belong in the text. In a couple of places I plagiarize a page or paragraph from my other books, but this collection is three-fourths brand new.

Nothing that follows will encourage you to look on the bright side, nor even on a conspiratorial dark side. There are more than enough books that encourage self-deception, both knowingly and unknowingly. I hope I am not deceiving myself that this is not one of them.

I

May You Have My Luck

THE TOPICAL MATTER THAT prompted this chapter was a defeat against insurmountably favorable odds, when victory could be reasonably regarded as in the bag—nope. When such happens you are not quite sure that the negative miracle did not occur because the gods were purposely out to get YOU: that you were not only jobbed but you had also been 'Jobed,' as in the Book of.[1]

There is an implicit optimism in the word *luck*. Unmodified, we supply the adjective *good*: naked luck means good luck. But then wouldn't it be my luck to put the lie to the unspoken hopefulness implicit in *luck* unmodified? For luck is as likely to be bad as good, rather more likely, you believe, if you are, like me, an historian and dispositionally a pessimist. Only the dimmest of cup-as-half-fullers, or experts in high finance of not-so-distant memory that brought about the fiasco of 2008 and who within ten years have forgotten any lessons that should have been learned from it and are already reproducing the conditions for an encore, could think that whatever goes up will not come down or suppress the thought that its very going up is what will bring it down. And in that debacle insurance companies, who owe their very existence to bad luck, led the pack of idiot optimists.

To real estate prices and stock indices, one might as well add sexual orgasm and illicit drugs. Highs lead to downs and letdowns. The question whether the hangover or posthigh depression was worth it is never really faced with a neutral disposition, because the timing of the evaluation bears mountains of determinative force. So it is not as if a stock market bubble is a bad thing for everyone. Those who have the luck to get in early and then get out before it pops are winners. Never mind that the losers outnumber them and that their losses are greater than the winners' gains; the losers discover that in effect they got Ponzied.

Luck has its own economics. Good and bad luck are connected in some strange way, so that one of them, the good, suggests the imminence (and immanence) of the other. Why, you may ask, do we go through that silly gesture of knocking on or touching wood or, if that seems a bit vulgar, finding ourselves inexplicably saying "knock on wood" or "touch wood" upon hearing good news or when we tell about some good thing that happened to fall our way?

Even a dyed-in-the-wool secular rationalist, every once in a while, banks on luck, as when he understands that he is taking a chance, or as he prefers to put it, undertaking a risk he deems worth taking. Such a type, though, may be less alert than the more overtly superstitious person to take care to husband his luck, for luck, the good kind, must be husbanded—not banked on in the sense of 'counted on,' but banked in the sense of 'saved up,' with its deployment deferred and economized. The lucky person knows not to press his luck, not to draw on it too often, nor to ask too much of it. It is as scarce as the courage of a United States senator.

Hitler made that mistake when his preternatural run of good luck lasting some twenty years, every improbability falling his way, lulled him into thinking that the stern law of limited good luck did not apply to him. He even, hubristically, let himself believe luck had nothing to do with it, that it was all attributable to his godlike genius. Nemesis, in his case, was only taking a long nap. Nothing angers the gods like presumption. Ask Ajax or Satan. That is why Jews never had baby showers, until recently, when we too succumbed to the complacency of that generic American optimism that doesn't bother to think that an unborn baby is an unhatched chicken that is being counted prematurely. I know that the enormous decline in infant mortality from what it was as few as a hundred years ago means that the need for apotropaic magic (the technical term for rituals we use to ward off evil or keep the demons at bay) is not as urgent as in days of yore, but do you really want to wake those black-humored gods by so presuming on their sleepiness and loss of power in that particular domain?

As I presently revise this chapter—its first iteration published before the Trump regime took power—more than a few Jews I know are keeping their passports on the night table, hiding some ready cash behind the books on the bookshelves, checking housing prices in places ranging from Canada to . . . ?[2] Incredibly some are even entertaining the thought of learning German.[3] Is there any place to go? Respectful piety, even if unfelt, for the fate of six million Jews has passed its use-by date, not just for old-style anti-Semites who simultaneously deny the Holocaust and celebrate it, but also for the British Labour Party and the ever-craven academic Left for whom courage takes the form of denying Israelis, even those who agree with them, invitations to conferences. This time the Jew is going to catch it from all sides, with Muslims joining Christians on the one issue they seem to agree on. The Jewish move since the late nineteenth century of faking right and going left won't work anymore, if it ever did. Sorry for that lament; the best luck the Jews ever had—America in the very decades I have lived the bulk of my life—has been too good to be true and its time is up. Should it strike you as strange that it is my good luck that motivates the bitterness of this paragraph?

Best to save up your portion of good luck, if you can, and though modesty, both false and true, might counsel you to attribute your successes to luck the better to quell the envy of your mates—"Gee, imagine, I got an A+, or in the United Kingdom, a first-class honors, dumb luck I guess"—you are wise to be crossing your fingers behind your back when you say that to avoid debiting too many good things to your good-luck account. Those moments of obligatory false modesty do not draw on your stores of luck all that much, you think, because you fervently believe that luck had nothing to do with your success. It was merely the natural outcome of your talents. But you might well be guilty of taking Luck's name in vain, and so even the social nicety of false modesty has costs you might not have fully appreciated.

There is an ancient pedigree to this kind of chariness about good fortune. Herodotus tells of one Polycrates (sixth century BCE), the tyrant of Samos, whose run of good luck became something of a byword in his own day—like Hitler's, too good not to elicit its own destruction

(3.39). This Polycrates, by the way, 2,600 years before the vogue of be-havioral economics, showed that what was common knowledge *then* could count as a prize-winning discovery *now* when he noted that he earned more gratitude from various friends he plundered by returning what he had taken from them than if he had never taken their property in the first place.

The luck of this man was so incredibly good that his formal friend and ally, the king of Egypt, Amasis II (d. 526 BCE), wrote to warn him of the divine retribution such luck would provoke and to take measures to defend himself against his own good luck. Luck like yours, he said, provokes the envy of the gods. "Better to go through life experiencing bad as well as good luck than to know nothing but success. I have never yet known nor heard tell of anyone who enjoyed a prosperity so total that he did not ultimately come to a bad end and lose everything that had previously sustained him" (3.40). Amasis counseled Polycrates to find the one object that was most precious to him, the thing it would most hurt him to lose, and to throw it away so that it could never be recovered.

Polycrates agreed with the wisdom of his friend's advice. He thought hard about which possession he would most regret losing and decided it was his richly jeweled signet ring. He boarded a ship, headed out to sea, and tossed the ring into the deep. You can guess what happened next. A fisherman catches a large fish, a delicacy fit for a king, too good to take to market, and instead presents it to Polycrates, his lord, as a gift. Polycrates is duly grateful, orders his cooks to prepare it, and when gutting the fish they find the ring and rush to take it to Polycrates. He, quite amazed, wastes no time in writing Amasis to tell him of this re-markable event, a happenstance against near-infinite odds. What does Amasis do? He renounces his friendship with Polycrates so as to avoid—somewhat strangely we moderns might think—"[having] to feel in his heart the pain that he would feel for a man who was his friend . . . when some great calamity did eventually befall Polycrates" (3.43). To Amasis, that surreal return of a beloved object sealed Polycrates's doom, and he was perhaps worried that he might get hurt with more than sorrow by the aftershocks of that doom if he were too closely associated with Polycrates. Sure enough, sometime later Polycrates was "butchered in a truly monstrous way . . . in a way too appalling for words." Herodotus is normally not reticent about providing such words. His *Histories* abound in horrific deaths and mutilations. We are left to the sickest reaches of our own imaginations to construct a death for Polycrates sufficiently gruesome to cancel out a lifetime of good fortune.

A story like this is too good to have escaped Montaigne, who notes how obviously ineffective the mere tossing away of a ring would be to "placate the turning of the Wheel of Fortune with such a carefully arranged disaster."[4] But he knows too that we will never cease attempting to manage our luck, to forfend both the evils of bad luck and, in Polycrates's case, the evils of good luck, even if we half know that our strategies and tactics are likely to have a low success rate. If we manage to rise above actually undertaking defensive rituals of various sorts, we still worry that we might have jinxed ourselves by being too rational (or lazy) not to have undertaken them.

Go to the experts on such matters. No one understands luck management better than soldiers under fire, who escape death by a gust of wind, by a timely occasion of enemy friendly fire wiping out its own troops as they are about to overrun the poor soldier's position, or at the whim of someone with a desk job who sends him to a quiet zone, or by the Bible in his chest pocket, stopping the bullet (with his name on it) right in the middle of the Book of Job. This is a frequent theme in soldier memoirs, as is equally that of a similar gust of wind or untimely friendly fire, or zigging when zagging would have been best, killing your mate or you.[5] Not all the memoir writers were lucky zaggers, though obviously most were. Some survived horrific disfiguring wounds and lived to write.

Vietnam vet Tobias Wolff astutely saw the fear that tormented him as economizing on his luck: "Fear won't always save you, but it will take some of the pressure off your luck."[6] Those minutes of respite from fear purchased by simple unwariness, a precious moment of miraculous fearlessness, draw down your finite amounts of luck and must be compensated for. So grim are the accounts that Luck kept that one North Vietnamese soldier reported that many of his comrades felt as if good things, "small acts of love," were "a bad omen, as though happiness must necessarily call down its own form of retribution in war."[7]

Luck and Fate are still deities we give some level of credence and deference to, though we may rechristen them as Providence or as

God's Plan, with secularists also refashioning grim necessity and perverse randomness by easy recourse to the reductionism supplied by
the Gene or the Market. Yet inscrutable Luck still wriggles its way in
to determine which gene you get and when you get in and out of the
market.

Mark VII, the pseudonym of Max Plowman, author of one of the
more powerful World War I memoirs—*Subaltern on the Somme*—notes
that the omnipresent lethal danger of battle suffused the simplest use
of the future tense with unintended irony, and with a whole lot of presumption. Any utterance that took the next half hour for granted de-
pleted your luck account by tempting the gods, or in his view Fate, to
do you in: "The cloud of uncertainty that hung above us every moment
while we were under fire, putting its minatory query before the least
anticipation, is lifted, and we are free to say 'In an hour's time,' without
challenging Fate with the phrase."[8]

Feeling lucky in that world is asking for it; the gods will nail you.
So too in our safe world, a world in which most of you, no differently
from me, hire substitutes for war, most of us nonetheless still feel we
must husband our luck. We cannot help ourselves. Feeling lucky comes
unbidden, as do the heebie-jeebies, which are to feeling lucky what bad
luck is to good luck. Strange it is, but feeling lucky itself often elicits
the heebie-jeebies, the niggling thought occurring that feeling lucky is
a diabolical setup, a trick.

Feeling lucky is a disturbance of the mind that makes us think something good awaits us if we take a chance, but that lucky feeling most
assuredly generates more false positives than true. The casino industry
depends on that. Nor, conversely, does every case of the heebie-jeebies
mean the plane you are boarding is going to crash. The heebie-jeebies
generate a lot of false positives. But not always: even the utterly rational
Horatio counsels Hamlet to heed his (5.2.213–14).

The perverse thing is that these uncanny feelings wreak havoc with
our virtue. If we heed them and defer flying, we should feel like a
coward or a nut. And if we do not heed them, and the plane does not
crash, we are hardly entitled to feel courageous, or even lucky. Yet we
have been known to congratulate ourselves on our brave overcoming
of a temptation to drop our sword and shield and flee to the rear in the
face of mouse or a bat. What fools the gods make of us.

Here is a story that should not seem strange to most of you. In it I worry about how my actions might affect not just my luck but the luck of the Green Bay Packers, if we allow that the two can be readily separable. This is a domain of not mere worry, but of hunches, inklings, qualms, and the heebie-jeebies. Substitute any team of your own choosing, or a competition such as an election you desperately care about—one in which, say, the handicappers predict your horse is 91% certain to win a mere three months before the election—and you will, I bet, have experienced similar anxieties about how to get a step up on or try to outsmart that Trickster we call God, Fate, Luck, the gods, or the Powers That Be (or if you were so complacent as not to have worried before the event, then not subsequently to feel guilt for your complacency having partly caused the debacle).

The year was 2011; the Packers were to play the Chicago Bears in Chicago in January, the winner to go to the Super Bowl. Tickets were going for about $900 online and I was wondering whether I should buy two, one also for my daughter Bess, a devoted fan. I began to deliberate: Would God punish the Packers because I was too cheap to spend $1,800 for such an important game shamefully watching in warmth for free on TV instead of sitting outside in the cold for nearly five hours? Or rather, would he punish them for my shallowness of soul that would let me frivolously spend that kind of money in the face of charitable causes I would not contribute to anyway, were I not to buy the tickets? But I, to tempt God all the more, told myself that if I did not go to the game and the Packers won I would give $1,800 to the local animal shelter, a charity that really does put serious pressure on me. I only have to glimpse one of their frequent emails picturing a forlorn dog dunning for a contribution and I click the Donate Now button and shell out.

While I was caught up in this quandary, I saw the dean of the law school walking down the hall. I decided to ask him what he would do. I said, "Evan, I need to ask your advice." He no doubt was a bit nonplussed, we not being especially close and I never having asked him for advice before. "Would you shell out $1,800 for two tickets to the Packer-Bear game this weekend?" He said, "No, I couldn't care less who wins that game." Evan, you see, is something of a literalist; I do not think he was meanly making me pay for not adding "if you were me" to my initial question. So I rephrased it. I knew him to be a crazed

UCLA fan, his undergrad alma mater, so I made the obvious substitution. "No, Evan," I said. "Suppose it were the Final Four of the college basketball tournament and UCLA were playing—would you spend that kind of money to go to the game, or would you think that you would either jinx them by spending it or jinx them by not spending it?" He paused for no more than three seconds—his usual style being to pause for weeks of thought—and then said firmly, "I would spend the money." "But," I said, "wouldn't you worry that you screwed them by that kind of wastefulness, its lack of seriousness, that you would anger some demonic forces?" His answer: "No, for then I would know that I had done all that I could possibly do."

I thought that answer truly inspired, an epiphany of vatic wisdom. Who would have thought he was so magically in touch with uncanny forces, as the perfect wisdom of his answer revealed? I immediately went back to my office and bought the tickets. The Packers, moreover, won, and went on to win the Super Bowl that year. Did I feel that I, or Evan, was part of the causal mechanism of their success? Well, a little bit, but not as much as I felt a part of the causal mechanisms that made them blow an insurmountable lead to Seattle in the championship game four years later in 2015, and I am still trying to figure out what I did then to anger the gods so greatly.[9]

If feeling lucky risks provoking the gods, what about hope? Feeling lucky should not be confused with hope. When you feel lucky, you are energized. It's mostly a good feeling. Hope, however, is a peculiar type of irrationality that often attends misery, and it is not so much the antithesis of despair as its fraternal twin, for the same misery can generate both. Hope is more decorous than feeling lucky, more modest, usually operating in a sadder terrain, it not even asking you to take a chance. Hope is that last fraying thread keeping you from slipping into the sludge of the Slough of Despond. You are feeling anything but lucky when hoping. Christianity made hope a theological virtue because it is hard to keep believing in a beneficent God when you are poor, sick, hungry, lame, and miserable. You are tempted, and fail on occasion to resist the temptation, to curse him, take arms against him and the sea of troubles you are now holding him accountable for. Up until very recently, had you lived in ancient, medieval, or early modern times, you were ever more likely to be cold and starving than being well fed near a warm fire. Year in and year out, if it were not one of the frequent famine years, the lords and church were skimming your surplus produce. Forget the added miseries of living in one of those regions where free companies or war bands were passing through plundering for provisions and raping for fun, and you were supposed to what? Hope? Is there any solace there?

Feeling lucky is something that even I, a pessimist, have felt not infrequently, but it does not lead me to bet double or nothing. Instead, it is experienced *after* the hopes I allow myself have not been dashed. I take care to make sure my feeling lucky is retrospective rather than prospective. It is the 'phew' or 'whew' that escapes your lips almost involuntarily when you make your connecting flight after taking off late. This kind of backward-looking feeling lucky thus merges with gratitude; it is a thank-you note to the Powers That Be for favors actually delivered. But the pleasantness of this kind of feeling lucky is somewhat marred by feeling foolish for all the expense of spirit lost in wasted worry. Moreover, this feeling foolish is not dispelled by the belief that had you not worried you would have provoked a contrary outcome.

One of the chief problems with hoping, small hopes no less than grand ones, is that it lets you down so often; so despite the fact that you felt lucky you made your connection, you recognize you have been engaged in hoping mostly when it ends in disappointment. Yet with the fading to black of small hopes, you do not sink into despair—even you recognize that the stakes are low—but into a kind of resignation, if, that is, you do not sink into a small rage fueled by frustration when, say, your flight is finally, after you have waited for seven hours, announced to have been canceled. But large hopes—an end to the evils of unmotivated cruelty, climate change, racism, irresponsible and corrupt government—are you kidding? One tries desperately to hope that in the end God will do justice, but that particular hope is, you know, a fond one and sends you deeper into despair. Strange, is it not, that Latin *hope*[10] seems naked in English if not prefixed with 'de' as in *(de)sperate* and *(de)spair*, the 'de' taking hope away, negating it.

One can wish, but wishing is something short of hope. I can sensibly wish for the impossible, but not sensibly hope for it, so that many of our large hopes are really just wishes. You know the odds are long when you hope; were they considerably better you would not be hoping; you would be expecting. But the danger is that an innocent wish can start you on the path to wishful thinking and self-deception. Jane Austen captures the progression perfectly: "what Marianne and her mother conjectured one moment, they believed the next—that with them, to wish was to hope, and to hope was to expect."[11]

Let us abandon hope (hope is what the Greeks understood to be the evil those black-humored gods left as a bad joke in Pandora's box) and test our luck instead. Luck has the allure of the primitive and the pagan lurking about it. Even God seems to give it space, a kind of liberty in the medieval sense, of being free of certain jurisdictional claims of a higher-up, in this case of God. He has put much of it beyond his control, delegating the workings of Luck to demons, gods, and sprites who are something less than all powerful, but powerful enough to ruin a picnic, and a life.

Luck, I have claimed, is felt to be allotted to us in finite quantities, and its finiteness makes a demand to husband it.[12] But our luck does not exist in a vacuum; its quality and quantity seem to be affected by the quality of other people's dealings with their luck. Your luck might very well mess with mine. Think how Caesar's luck turned Pompey's incredibly good luck in the opposite direction. On the brighter side, your bad luck could very well be my good luck.

Obviously that is the case when you and I face off in a zero-sum situation, where your good luck necessarily is the same as my bad luck. The very grim consequence is that you can hoard your luck all you want and still have someone take it away from you. (We will return to this issue in the next chapter.)

There is a Bemba proverb that the anthropologist Max Gluckman put into circulation more than half a century ago: "To find one beehive in the woods is good luck, to find two is very good luck, to find three is witchcraft."[13] At best, your neighbors will compel you to share your find; at worst, they will kill you, not just for hoarding honey but for using up everyone else's good luck. The Bemba thus, with crystalline precision, capture another aspect of Polycrates's bind. You need fear not only the envy of the gods but also that of your fellow human competitors for that scarce resource we call good luck. It is not the gods who kill Polycrates; in fact, they take care to send warning dreams to his daughter to urge him to avoid accepting an invitation to visit the man who will gruesomely murder him (3.124).

I can imagine some paint-by-numbers evolutionary psychologist inventing an explanation for the adaptability of envy and its cousin Schadenfreude. One theory might go like this: Our ancestors lived in conditions of great scarcity; it took the agricultural and industrial revolutions before people could envisage that economies could grow, the pie get bigger. Before then, if someone took too big a share of the communal pie or captured too much of nature's good things, or was too good a hunter and did not share his kill, well then everyone was worse off for his being better off. To hell with skills qualifying him for survival of the fittest; his loser cavemates had the embryos of Schadenfreude and envy growing in them and killed the good hunter. So we get norms of sharing enforced by fear, and the survival of the less fit assured by our less fit ancestors banding together out of sheer annoyance at the big man's success.[14]

Who knows? Stories like that are a dime a dozen these days, without proof or any explanatory value whatsoever. You could easily retell the story I just told, it being no more or less convincing, with a twist. Instead of killing the lucky hunter or honey finder, the have-nots worship him as a god. No envy at all; they prefer desperately (there is that luckless word again) to find shelter in his good luck. They will serve him and make offerings to him if he will only smile upon them now and then.

There are still other stories. We also have the sneaky feeling that both good luck and bad luck are contagious. Early medieval war leaders, if they won a few battles at the start of their careers, would get a reputation for being lucky, and people would flock to them to join up. Their enemies would quail, fearing they were up against more than a mere human. Good luck bred more of the same, until it got too good to be true, for soon it ran up against the problem of diminishing returns. A bigger force of followers meant you needed to capture ever more to keep them happy with distributions of plunder and lands. But all the low-hanging fruit had already been picked; you now needed to mount more costly expeditions to find unplundered people to keep your pie growing. Inevitably it cost too much to make the pie bigger and then it would start to get smaller as your men would cut better deals with new lucky upstarts. Your luck had run out, done in by its very success.

Unless, that is, you turned on your followers, close at home, and started to plunder them. That was a forerunner of what we might call taxation, and it is part of the story of state formation, put in such a way that would strike a chord with antitax libertarian types, who have yet to imagine what it meant to live in the path of competing warlords, and assume the peace that allows them to hold on to what they call their property does not need to be paid for. Achieving peace is expensive, maintaining it equally so; it requires law and armies, neither of which come cheaply.

If good luck can be at times contagious, bad luck is virulently so. Once you get a reputation for being accident prone or for merely not having things ever go your way, people start to brand you a loser. Being kind enough to stay friends with such a poor unfortunate soul is costly, for others will abandon you for not abandoning him. Do you want your daughter to go on a date with someone who, when driving, has been smashed into three times in the last year, each accident not in the least his fault?

Borrowing from Claudius's description of love, we might say:

> There lives within the very flame of [good luck]
> A kind of wick or snuff that will abate it;
> And nothing is at a like goodness still;
> For goodness, growing to a pleurisy,
> Dies in his own too-much. (4.7.113–17)

Good luck dies in its own "too-much." But does bad luck die in its own too much? Not on your life (or your death); it seems to grow geometrically, its interest compounding and compounding. The math of good luck is a matter of simple subtraction (and addition), the math of the bad exponential. Bad luck grows like an especially dreaded instance of itself: *cancer*, those amazingly healthy, gifted, and energetic cells that keep on reproducing and reproducing, having found, perversely but not incorrectly, the fountain of youth, forever renewing themselves. But cancer's good luck, though it be your bad luck, is also, in the end, its own bad luck, for as soon as it kills its host, call him 'you,' it too must die in its own too-much, at least at that one particular site.

I cannot tell you how worn my knuckles are by knocking on wood for "earning" (that's in scare quotes) a law professor's salary teaching Icelandic sagas (and property). I fear it might all be a setup, even though I have nearly made it home safely, having reached age seventy-four suffering only the usual loss of physical and mental acuity that comes with old age. But the luck of not dying young means experiencing the debilities of old age, the punishment for the luck of having reached it. That good luck of us oldsters is nothing but bad luck for the generation of our children and grandchildren as we consume the scarce resources that are thus denied them, let alone the debts we have pushed off on to them.

Some of you might be familiar with the Yiddish mantra, a third German, two-thirds Hebrew—*keinahora* (meaning "no evil eye")—said to defend against compliments and good wishes and occurrences of good luck. Should someone praise the beauty of your child or her intelligence, or congratulate you on your newborn baby, you must hurry to ward off the evil eye and say *keinahora*. The kind and wise congratulator of the newly delivered mother knows well enough only to whisper a blessing in the mother's ear lest it provoke the demons who are surely trying to catch what is being said in order to blast the infant and make the mother doubt the very intentions of the congratulator.

There is an extraordinary *narcissism of negativity* in such beliefs. By that somewhat pretentious phrase I mean to indicate the frequent and intrusive sense that the entire universe seems to have singled you out, little old you and me, to screw us. So cosmically significant are you and I that our mere wishes and hopes have, we feel, an extraordinary causal power to generate bad things, but that power is resistant to my or your efforts to direct it in a reliable way. The joke on us is that that power invariably operates perversely. No tactic that works once to counter the perversity of fortune is more than randomly likely to work again.

Sometimes our narcissism of negativity goes to sleep and lets us live less worriedly. We enter a state of reasonably relaxed unwariness, which might pass for something approaching a sense of well-being. Our guard is down, but our very complacency will provoke the demons, the gods, Nemesis, or God. A tale to show what I mean: I dread most all occasions called parties and claim I have come down with a migraine to excuse my failure to attend. How could I so presume on the emptiness of the heavens? The lie has a will of its own and flies off to awaken the gods and rat me out. The little winged lie points to me as its father and points them at me. Thus does my lie work as the generator of its own punishment, a small Dantesque *contrapasso*,[15] the migraine hitting me at home exactly when I should be ringing the host's doorbell. I end up having told the truth.

The joke is on me. Luck jokes abound. There is one embedded in the curse that is the title of this chapter: May you have my luck. That it is meant as a curse IS the joke. Its genius is that it transforms a kvetch into a malediction, self-mockery into hostility, and, with a little bit of luck, it is self-deprecating enough to spare its author the revenge of its target.

2

The Law of Conservation of Good Things

IN THE PREVIOUS CHAPTER I noted that good luck and bad luck are often locked in a zero-sum game, not just between individuals, as when your good luck is my bad luck, but also for each individual across time. That was one of the main points of Herodotus's story of Polycrates and of those rituals meant to ward off the evil eye prompted by one's good fortune. But zero sum is not quite accurate, for if good fortune tends to be equalized, with your account ending up balanced at zero (if you are lucky), the principle of equalization does not seem to apply to ill fortune with compensatory good canceling the usual bad stuff. The direction over time is downward, or if we take the measure at any one time, the bad will tend to outweigh the good, if not for the individual, then for the world at large. Remember there are two kinds of math at play, one putting a cap on the good, the other allowing for endless expansion of evil.

But how seriously are we to take this pessimistic view, which is so frequently felt if not quite believed as a rational matter? It is easy to refute the general applicability of the balancing of accounts over the lifetime of individuals. Some people so obviously have it better than others, and no grand principle of justice does any evening out, unless we cheat and make mere mortality, death itself, the final balancing of everyone's account at zero, working as relief for those with nothing but bad luck and as a comeuppance, an axe in the head, for those who lived fortunate lives.[1]

The creation of heaven and hell is in part an attempt to rectify the unjust earthly imbalance where the evil thrive and the good die young by overrewarding good with an eternity of bliss and overpunishing evil with an eternity of torment. Forget for the moment that those suffering good people, while living, must hope that the promissory note of bliss after death will be honored. Even if the paper is good, a massive imbalance of good and evil still remained at the global level since so few were saved compared with the multitudes damned, given that no matter how good a person might be, he might end up in Christian hell for making it into Muslim heaven; could his soul be in two places at once? Being saved in one of these religions generally damned you, with rare exception, in the other. A righteous pagan or two might be allowed a pass—those souls, for instance, who never knew of the faith or could possibly have known of it because they lived before Christ or Mohammed. These had a better chance to be granted admission than those who knew of it and rejected it, no matter how virtuous, by neutral lights, they might have been.

In the Christian dispensation one could easily get the sense that the population density was greater in hell than in heaven; no biblical text limited admission to hell, as Revelation could be seen to limit the seats in heaven to 144,000 (Rev. 7.4, 14.1–3). Purgatory worked to open the gates for a few more who could make recompense by enduring purging fire, it differing from infernal fire only in that it had an endpoint. One way to make sure the number of saved was greater than the number damned was to let everyone in. The idea of universal salvation surfaced in the early days of the church, though it was soon condemned as heretical.[2] Nonetheless, a stake could not quite be driven into its heart. Universalism had something of a heyday in nineteenth-century America, an honorable forerunner of the less honorable American self-esteem movement, which I think can be justly seen as its deformed earthly successor.

What about at the cosmological level? The pre-Socratic Greeks were primed for zero-summing: they saw payback and getting even—in other words, justice—as the organizing principle of the cosmos as well as of the human moral and social worlds. Thus winter gets even with summer, summer with winter, night with day, hot with cold, dry with moist. Conflict, payback, and balance are the organizing creative principles.[3] Not just early Greek cosmology understood the natural order as a struggle for evenness and balance; local portions of our modern cosmology do too, as in Newton's third law of motion. When I hit my forehead as a gesture of my own stupidity, my hand is paid back in kind by my forehead, which hits my hand no less forcefully, every action generating its equal and opposite double. The explosion of powder that sends a bullet whistling to its target pushes back as hard against your hand or shoulder and the gun itself; luckily the force is less focused but it adds up to the same amount. Add too the law of conservation of energy that can be seen as formalizing the idea of what goes around comes around: in a closed system, the total energy of the system is conserved, that is, it remains a constant.

To what extent do we assume that certain dispositions, emotions, or motivational and psychological states, not just luck, are conserved—if you suppress a little here, does the equivalent pop up somewhere else? But as suggested in the first paragraph of this chapter, this conservation seems only to govern things we think of as good. Good things have at best a fixed supply; use up some of it and either you or others will have to pay for that good. Bad things, alternately, apparently can create themselves out of nothing, *ex nihilo*, depleting none of that infinite store of bad things. Those bad things still remain fully available to work their harm. You cannot evade this sentiment by declaring bad things to be a feature of God's unfathomably benevolent plan, nor by fiat supply him with infinite goodness that overwhelms what seems to be infinite evil. He has yet to prove that this view is only making excuses either for his lack of power against evil or because he, more sinisterly, chooses to hoard his infinite good and not dispense it, because he likes the imbalance the way it is. This latter view complicates the claim of God's benevolence.

I am talking about beliefs. I am not sure—no I am sure—that there is no way one could actually add up the good and evil in the world.[4] I am only trying to get at how deep the view is that bad outweighs good, and that what good there is, is 'conserved,' fixed in supply, as we saw in the previous chapter with good luck. In homage to this pessimism, websites abound detailing luridly the bad endings of Powerball and Mega Millions lottery winners, dead by overdoses, murdered by envious relatives, or swindled out of the rest. Count yourself lucky for losing.

Notice too the common belief, old as the hills, that the virtue pie keeps getting smaller from one generation to the next: our grandparents were thus more courageous and honorable than we are, were less promiscuous, and they could not match their parents, who thought your grandparents had not measured up much either. People were surely tougher back then. They had to be. Pain was not optional in the days of old as it has become in our time in the rich West. And even aspirin only became readily available at the end of the nineteenth century. The remnant of small virtue I manifest by not seeking out a willing physician to prescribe fentanyl for my arthritic knees is canceled by my lack of virtue when I tediously complain about the pain I am not very stoically enduring.

Though surely those people in the old days could be as vain as we are, their vanity did not have the assist of the technology that yields selfie narcissism, or enhancement and reconstructive surgeries for a new and better plastic you, nor did they elect a grotesque Vice of Vanity as their president (Louis XIV was not elected by the people). Instead of having Dorian Gray front for us, which would have been bad enough, we have his picture doing the fronting, the truth of the portrait not even hidden in an attic but in plain view for all to see. The horror is that his portrait is a mirror held up to reveal the truth of our own deeply shallow self-defining self-involvement. Trump is our truth, more than Nero was ever Rome's.[5] (Topical references like this are not a good idea for by the time the book is published the event or person has passed into oblivion. But unfortunately this reference, I bet, will have a substantial half-life. I will take a pass on coronavirus though, in hopes it will pass me by, otherwise this small volume will hit the press posthumously.)

In every age the old think everything is going to hell, that the young have given up on all virtue, that there was some golden age in the past. So much folk wisdom or folk imbecility subscribes to some form of this belief, and why should I claim to be immune from the predictable lifecycle determinants of my glum view of the present? Myth and unreason it all may be, but it holds more than a few of us in its grip, even though we know we are acting out a well-known script. But for every exceptional divinely inspired Jeremiah with proof from God that things really were going to hell for Judeans, if not Babylonians (more conservation at work), who is wrongly ignored, there is the conventional lamenter rightly ignored. I am singing the same tired tune sung by geezers of old. I suppose they too were not unaware of the conventional role they were playing and thus felt obliged to add what soon became a conventional preface to the conventional lament: "but this time it really *is* different."

Thus, the United Kingdom and the United States really *are* in self-destructive death spirals (those two are not polities like Hungary or Romania, where death spirals are the norm), and for all its sins and imperfections that Anglo-American world was mostly (let's not fight about this) a good thing. This time, two or three of the horsemen seem to have already passed by: climate change with attendant species die off; the disappearing act of honey bees, more than just symbols of virtue. Add the growing strength of nativist genocidal ideologies which, unlike their 1930s' versions in which murderous visions mostly topped out at a really nice pogrom (it seems few people counted, even if they knew about it, what the Turks had already done to the Armenians), today's adherents know exactly what it led to and want a redo. If it is possible to be more morally defective than the Nazis of the 1930s, our own white supremacists and neo-Nazis might have made the grade.

So deep does the idea of conservation of the good run that we need not invoke the pre-Socratics; we can turn to the highest and ablest Christian authority. The decorous St. Thomas Aquinas (d. 1274), following the less decorous Tertullian (d. 240 CE), understood the pleasure of heaven to need the suffering of the damned in hell, heaven being arranged in Tertullian so as to provide unobstructed sightlines for the blessed to witness what they were being spared.[6] Better not get bored by the sight and site of woe, despite the imaginativeness of the devils at coming up with new horrors and torments to keep piquing your interest, almost giving Stalin, Hitler, Mao, and Pol Pot runs for their money.

One will probably not tire of that infernal spectacle as fast as one will tire of the mandatory singing of hosannas in that timeless heavenly world. Suppose, though, one of the elect should come to find it all wearisome, especially since he thinks he recognizes his mother or daughter down there. Does boredom then become a sin as dark as Satanic pride, and can boredom get you cast down to play your part in the pit? Or is my thinking that boredom might even be possible in a timeless heaven a sure sign of my worse-than-fallen nature? Heaven is timeless and boredom is so dependent on its connection to the experience of time passing, in boredom's case, not passing quickly enough, but going ever so slowly. Yet maybe perfect boredom is best achievable in a timeless heaven, with time having come to a full stop. As has been long recognized, salvation would have to give the elect a new psychology that eliminates the capacity for boredom, such psychology inconceivable to blinkered sublunary sorts as me, a psychology that would, think of it, put most of the entertainment business out of business.

Both Christ and Mary possess a Plenitude of Grace. Their good is by this doctrine made never exhaustible; it is always full to the brim no matter how often drawn upon. The doctrine has half an eye turned to the insistent anxiety not only that good things are limited but also, even grimmer, that depletability is a necessary characteristic of the good. Why attach this doctrine to Christ and Mary? Because, it seems, the very suggestion of their humanity brings with it the idea of necessary limits on their good, the idea of the corruption or the corruptibility of fallen flesh, and the necessary evil that defines what it means to be human, which evil, to speak truth, is less attributable to our flesh, than to our 'spirit,' to our defective souls.[7]

Good things bear a kind of poison in the gift, not just a string attached to it but an adamantine chain, the poison being that a gift comes burdened with a demand for requital. A gift imposes a near-absolute obligation on the recipient to make a return. Treat yourself to these philological coincidences that capture this deep ambivalence of gifts. In German *das Gift* means *poison*, thus generating a cross-linguistic pun to capture one of the truisms of the anthropology and sociology of gift exchange, which marches to a similar rhythm I am positing for good luck: getting even. And what is the most common Old Norse word for *luck*? *Gæfa,* which is also cognate with our word *gift*, *give*. A gift MUST be paid back: that is the poison in it. The German and English *gift* and Norse *gæfa* share a common etymological root; *they are the same word*. Gift, luck, and poison are all part of the same gift-wrapped package. (To add to the fun, Old Norse *gipt*, sometimes spelled *gift*, means not only gift but also marriage, wedding, the woman being given over.)

So how did *gift* end up meaning *poison* in German? Apparently from the idea of 'giving a dose' of medicine (medicine so closely annexed to poison), for 'dose' itself derives from the Indo-European root that means to give, yielding such cognates as *donation* and obviously French *don*, *donner*.[8] Add this: not only nice gifts required requital, so did bad ones, like an insult, or a harm. The Icelanders of the sagas well understood that revenge is merely the return of a 'favor' of negative value.[9]

One dominant stream in Christian theology put payback at its very core. Why, for instance, were the Incarnation, and the Crucifixion, necessary? Because mankind needed to make amends to compensate for the wrong Adam and Eve did God by their first disobedience. All humanity (despite the inherent 'dignity' we now ascribe to it) was not worthy enough or of high enough status to pay adequate compensation to satisfy God's claim against us; only God's Son was of adequate standing to pay himself over to make suitable amends for the wrong done the Father.[10] Only the Divine in one form could make atonement for a wrong done the Divine in another. Atonement? The very root of that word is to be 'at one,' the payback restoring a prior unity, making one whole again, unified by reconciliation, because the debt has been paid back, that is, satisfied.[11]

Again, as a hedge, before we deal with more specific examples, the conservation of good is not about truth but about a set of common, nearly ineradicable beliefs, which nonetheless have the 'ring' of truth, at least to those of a mildly pessimistic disposition. Obviously not all pies are the same size. Some are bigger than others, and we also know the same pie can get bigger or smaller over time,[12] that there can be good times and bad times that do not zero out. Gross domestic product can shrink or grow, and some social scientists claim to measure such things as happiness and show it rising or falling. Those suspect studies (I think they originate in a department of my university[13]) purport to rank nations on their happiness and usually end up making Danes or other very reserved dour Nordics the happiest people on earth. For an average Dane, I guess, it helps knowing everyone else thinks you are better looking than the average member of their own ethnic group. But then how much does being a happy Dane depend on knowing you are not a miserable Hungarian or Rwandan or Syrian, that a good part of blond blitheness is funded in the same way that the felicity of the blessed is funded: by looking at the charred and scarred damned as they writhe in hell? Even a businessman, who in one part of his brain knows that business in general can be good or bad for an entire economy or for a sector within an economy, can see things in the zero-sum way. Babbitt's close friend, Paul Riesling, does: "But what's the use of it? You know, my business isn't distributing roofing—it's principally keeping my competitors from distributing roofing."[14]

Whole peoples are consistently luckier than other peoples. Compare, for instance, the English with the Irish. Yet, we can amuse ourselves with the thought that the Brexiting Brits will end up zeroing out their long run of good luck with a bit of help from the costs of winning two world wars. Who knows, but soon the Irish will not only be hating the English but also be gloating at being richer, incredible as that may seem.

If an external enemy does not arise to take down a person or a whole nation, people are pretty good at self-destruction, at declining and falling. At least warlike Germanic tribes assisted Roman sybaritism and incompetent emperors, and then it still took a millennium for the empire, as Byzantium, to cease to matter significantly. America, on the other hand, fell to fears of an invasion of Guatemalan hotel maids. The fall of the western Roman Empire is a grand story by any estimation; the American fall, a bad and sad joke. Very sad.

It is easy to end up ranting, easy to sink into bitterness, but let me calm down and further examine the matter at hand. Return to the suggestion I made about the happiness of the Danes being at least in part constituted by knowing that they are not Hungarians. What makes anyone think happiness is always, or even mostly, an innocent sentiment? How willing are you to vouch for the moral quality of your happiness and joy and its accompanying smiles and laughter?[15] Smiles are often threatening, and smirks are smiles too. And the sweetness of laughter? It can register the torture of being tickled as well as the delight we take in someone else's discomfiture. Laughter is as often a sign of total craziness as it is of good adjustment, for we must evaluate each laugh as to the appropriateness of what elicited it, and the propriety of its volume, pitch, duration, and style. A laugh is often forced, as we well know, so it is hardly even a serviceable indicator of joy or even of minimal amusement. Take students laughing at a professor's lame joke, one of mine perhaps. They might only be trying to be nice; more likely they are trying to save the discomfort of their own embarrassment by saving me from mine were no one to laugh; or they are just being sycophantic.

Some might be stupid enough to think I was funny, the ones who, most likely, also get a big kick out of Bud Lite commercials. When you watch a comedy by yourself, how rare it is to burst out laughing, but when watching with another we laugh whenever they do and even when they do not but we expect we are supposed to anyway, lest we be impolite, lest we look like we are judging the other to be dimwitted because they either recommended the movie or have already laughed at jokes in it you did not find the least bit funny.[16] Do you get self-conscious over how much of your laughter is forced, is purely obligatory? Do you start feeling not just awkward, but craven? Do you start downgrading the intelligence of your colleagues because of their laughing at another colleague's attempt at wit in a faculty meeting? Do you begin to question friendships?

Step safely back from the threatening smile, or the contempt of the smirk, and merely consider that mindless grin of conversational engagement. As soon as you become aware of it, your face might start to ache, but if you wipe it off you will break the rules of conversational small talk, and even alarm or insult your interlocutor. We see then that the conventional facial and social markers of happiness, joy, and well-being are loaded and can mean a variety of things, often their opposite. These expressions are something like the auto-antonyms that are the subject of the epilogue (chapter 9).

Look how the sum of happiness is constituted. What portion of it comes in the form of Schadenfreude, the pleasure and delight we take in other people's unhappiness or misfortune? Happy people need not be so nice, some not insignificant portion of their happiness being parasitical on the misery and failures of others. A commonly told story, attributed to various Slavic peasant cultures,[17] captures a near universal of the emotional economy of roughly egalitarian communities, in which where you stand relative to the other members of the group means more to you than just about anything. The story goes like this: A genie offers a Ukrainian peasant anything he could want on one condition, that his neighbor get twice as much. The peasant thinks for a moment, and then makes his wish: "take out one of my eyes." We might smile, even laugh, but the smile would be a nervous one because the motivation that drives the peasant is so readily understandable. Better to be first in the smaller pond, but the only pond that matters to you, than to be last but significantly better off materially in the way utilitarian or a conventional economic rationality would recommend. One of the key measures of where you stand is if you can see that others envy you and you can indulge your contempt for them, envy being, strangely, one of the sincerest forms, because painful, that 'respect' can take. And that makes you happy.

A Sicilian proverb captures these thoughts even more brutally: *Nella stessa faccia, l'occhio destro odiava il sinistro*—"In the same face, the right eye hated the left."[18] This saying emphasizes the boundedness of the 'game,' the closeness of the competitors, and the rough egalitarianism that is a prerequisite for being a player. King Arthur thought he undid the conditions for such hostility among his knights with a round table. No, he did not. (We will return to the inadequacy of the round table more fully in the next chapter.) Relative standing in a closed system, of which human society offers many such fields of play, is what constitutes so much of our sense of well-being, or of chagrin, whether in the family, playground, workplace, profession, or house of worship.

What is one of the pleasanter joys than the glorying and exultation in the defeat of one's foes? And these foes may not have to have suffered defeat at your hands. When the Dallas Cowboys, say, lose to anyone, especially to teams they were expected to beat, I rejoice. The foe for such purposes may even be a friend, a colleague whose reputation seems to be doing a little better than one's own. We do not want our friends doing too much better than we are doing; we probably prefer that they do a tiny bit worse, only a tiny bit, with an occasionally good thing happening to them, such as the birth of a child. A good third of the Psalms subscribe to the ethics of the Slavic peasant story in some form.[19]

Most comedy, from Shakespeare to sit-com fare, is about making other people look like asses. Comedy, even more than tragedy, has revenge at its core, revenge, after all, being a kind of comic justice, a happy ending. Shakespeare's most disproportionate revenges are meted out less in tragedies like *Titus Andronicus* than in what Feste and Maria arrange for Malvolio in the best of Shakespeare's comedies: *Twelfth Night*. Feste, in agreement with the pre-Socratics, takes revenge to be an organizing cosmic principle: "And thus the whirligig of time brings in his revenges" (5.1.369–70). The *Merchant of Venice* is a comedy too, the joy (and funding) of the happy newly married couples at the end coming at Shylock's expense, paying him back for even daring to think of carving a pound of flesh out of that good man, the Jew-baiter Antonio, who, moreover, regularly, would spit on him and kick him. "I am as like . . . to spet on thee again, to spurn thee, too" (1.3.140–41).[20]

We need not invoke comedy and tragedy but that aspect of the entertainment industry we call the news. For decades moralists of various stripes and levels of sophistication have found television news troublesome, it, in effect, seating us in a virtual coliseum—viewer discretion advised—not unlike the blessed in heaven, watching people starving, beaten, bombed, murdered, driven from homes by the weather or by other humans. This 'entertainment' can hardly give rise to joy and happiness, except in morally defective souls, but it surely is not meant to make you miserable either or ruin your appetite, for dinner, back in the day, was soon to follow; today, we are often snacking as we watch anyway. At a minimum, the suffering depicted offers the satisfaction of counting our blessings (and thereby cautioning us not to count *on* our blessings, for as we saw that might activate Nemesis to visit upon us some compensating misfortune). Much of the pleasure offered comes in the form of *relief* captured by the thought that "there but for the grace of God go I," which has a cousinship with Schadenfreude, for the feeling is equally dependent on contrasting one's own fortune with that of more unfortunate others. Schadenfreude hardly need only manifest itself as exultant glee or, more quietly, with a smirk of satisfaction; it also finds a small home in relief as well as in some forms of pity.

Despite the veneer of pious gratitude that comes with "there but for the grace of God go I," we are entertained. The Schadenfreude is given proper muted dress; we do not gloat, but our attention is captured, and having one's attention engaged, while confident of one's own safety, is a pleasure, like the pleasure of reading a crime novel. It shares traits with the rubbernecking we find impossible to resist when driving by a road accident.

That is enough to make a strong claim for recognizing the Schadenfreude component of those 'positive' emotions happiness and joy.[21] It would be cheating to declare by fiat that the happiness that is Schadenfreude, or the happiness of ranking higher than your colleague or neighbor, is an entirely different emotion from virtuous happiness, sharing nothing with the more innocent joy of, say, being alive on a beautiful day with a full stomach. Sorry, but they are facets of the same 'happiness and joy syndrome,' only that the joy of being alive on a beautiful day might not be as enlivening as is the joy in the defeat of our foes were we worthy of having foes, blandly safe as we are. Instead, we must find an unworthy substitute for the defeat of a foe in that small grin we quickly suppress when we learn that a beheadphoned texter got hit by a car—no, not seriously injured, just bruised up enough to give him a wake-up call. The game I am playing here, only partly tongue-in-cheek, should nonetheless give us enough of an uneasy feeling that it might not be pure foolishness to think of happiness as subject to conservation, similar to the way that good luck is held to be by widespread folk belief.

Consider the emotional relief I brought up when discussing the news and the "there but for the grace of God go I" sentiment. If some not insignificant portion of happiness is Schadenfreude, then another rather significant portion of it is nothing more than relief. The word *relief* governs two somewhat distinct sentiments, as Jon Elster pointed out several decades ago: the feeling attendant when pain or misery ceases and the sensation when expected bad things do not materialize.[22] For this discussion we can lump them together, for they both generate what can pass for joy or happiness—indeed, *overjoyed* is the term we often apply to the sensation of a threatened bad thing not materializing. The 'over' in that joy is a function partly of the rebound effect. It turns out that the mole you were sure was a melanoma was only the standard kind of skin blotch that makes old skin so oppressively ugly. Oh joy, oh rapture unforeseen. The relief! Even the pleasure of sexual orgasm is nine-tenths relief, not of the kind of a threatened misfortune not materializing unless, if a male, its prematurity was the threat, but of the kind one gets when a boil pops or one stops banging a head against the wall, that is, when something unpleasant or excruciating ceases. But you can see what I am driving at. The pleasure in either of these cases is a function of the pleasure's relation to some kind of opposite, to a corresponding negation, and so we have yet again a tendency toward the conservation of pleasure, joy, or happiness. So utilitarianism's greatest happiness for the greatest number has some problems: it seems to forget that, by the account I am giving, the best that that 'greatest' can be is to get to zero, and the greater it gets, the more 'funding' it must find. Might that not be one of the drives toward imperialism? If this is not exactly true, it sure captures the gist of our deepest folk beliefs.[23]

I have one more wrinkle to add, one that got me started thinking about the subject of this chapter. In my book on disgust I devoted some eight pages to a discussion of Norbert Elias's views on the civilizing process in which feelings of disgust and shame, he argued, come to colonize new areas and make certain behaviors taboo that before the seventeenth century were supposed routine and okay, like blowing your nose on the tablecloth, not suppressing burps and farts, and not caring all that greatly about privacy in matters of excretion or sex.[24] His story borrows heavily from Freudian ideas of sublimation and repression, which also, as has been commonly noted, play according to a law of conservation (repress a desire or a drive here and it pops up as a neurosis there). But Elias gives the impression that there was an expansion of the amount of disgust in the social world that worked to suppress bawdier and rowdier medieval behaviors.

For the sake of argument, I asked if there was more disgust available in the seventeenth century than in the Middle Ages. Did it increase with the extension of the notion of good and bad 'taste'—that type of taste, not tongue centered, but governed by a susceptibility to finding oneself disgusted by vulgarity, by unstylish clothing or lack of 'refinement,' but mostly by failures of the new eating and excretory niceties? I offered an account that could be seen as an argument for conservation. It was that disgust did not so much increase as shift some of its terrain, with the shift in notions of what was the proper domain of cleanness or purity, not that there was an increase in the total disgust supply. Cleanness shifted from more a matter of one's ritual status, inner being, virtue and piety, and purity of soul to matters more of soap and water. This, however, should not be overstated: it might be a near human universal from ancient Sumer to saga Iceland to an American middle school that people sneer at another's form of dress and dirtiness however their conception of dirtiness might be constituted, for these things were markers of rank and status. An example from today will better capture what I mean about the possible conservation of disgust. Compare the person revolted both at the thought of eating a Big Mac and by those who eat them with the corresponding view of the Big Mac eater for the vegan, netting out at some kind of zero of two strongly opposing disgusts, each new disgust generating its corresponding conserving mechanism.

Let me reiterate that I do not want to push any of this too far. But what I will stand by is how deeply we feel that a law of conservation might well be at work in moral and social domains, where piety demands we think less of payback and more of the possibility of plenitudes of virtue, good, and happiness. Miserable experience suggests otherwise. Thus the resigned acceptance of the proverb that "only the good die young" along with the vulgar saying "shit happens," not "good things happen," or if they do, they will be paid for by shit happening. There is not even an available bodily substance or body part on the good side to oppose to 'shit' happening—'eyes,' 'muscles,' 'digesting stomach acid' happen? Nothing works. Milk? Nope. The purest moral bodily substance, tears, cannot work either; even if tears of joy are possible, tears of joy are an exception to the usual emotions tears stand for, and even when they are of joy, they are often of that joy that is the relief of having escaped some impending misfortune.

If we try to look on the bright side, we can claim that if the system is a closed one, then misery should also be conserved. But we know that is not true; only good things seem to be. When humans are involved, the system is never closed for bad things—for good things and for nicely motivated happiness, yes, but not for evil, which can grow and expand, not one whit at its own expense.

But, you say, surely technology and the advance of medical science give us healthier, longer, easier lives. Yes, true, I answer, no doubt health is a good thing, especially when it lets the young live productively during their useful years. But you also have to discount for the rather mixed blessing of long life—ever more mixed the longer it lasts—that comes along for the good health ride. Nor do technological advances only occur in the health field. They also occur in the unhealthy fields of lethal technology. I am truly grateful that the internet lets me sit in the bathroom accompanied by a library of books and articles measured in the millions. But, narrow self-interest aside, I doubt that that quite balances against what the internet has done for the resurgent healthiness of homicidal ideologies that make the excesses of the Inquisition look like child's play, though the horrors of the wars of religion in the sixteenth and seventeenth centuries can still hold their own in that diabolical, but all too human, competition, a game we might call: "Worst century ever: does any beat the twentieth?" Some might argue that the second half of the twentieth, surely in the West (thus putting Pol Pot, the Cultural Revolution, and Rwanda out of the calculus), was arguably the best of times anywhere ever for a larger percentage of people. Does that heavenly second half thus lower the unfathomable horror of the first half to levels that, if not reaching zero, at least give other centuries a chance in the game? Not on your life. Nor do this game's rules allow for adding in the joys of the anti-Semites or the Japanese rapists of Nanking in its first half, because the game is about the 'worst' century, not about whether miseries and antithetical joys sum out at zero. Not even the Black Death of the mid-fourteenth century gives the twentieth a run because with the subsequent shortage of humans in its second half, working people saw their wages rise substantially. They benefited from the bright side of levels of mortality probably never seen before and certainly never seen since. I have not said "never to be seen again" lest I count a diabolical changeling chicken before it has hatched. In the plague's defense too, human evil had a negligible lethal input (except, as usual, for Jews who got killed in various places for causing plague), that being carried out by the bacillus *Yersinia pestis*, which was innocently doing what a good *Y. pestis* does.[25]

"Name the worst century" is a game some historians in their cups might entertain themselves with in a pub. Offers one, "How about Attila or Genghis and various steppe peoples butchering their way westward every couple of centuries?" "Dealing with those sweet-hearted Romans," says another, "particularly given the Roman cruelty to animals to add to the mix?" The trouble is, with the Romans controlling so many centuries of history, it is hard to pick one.

Just think, though, that like Miniver Cheevy "who loved the days of old," you fantasize yourself gloriously performing in some grand earlier age. Then think how high the odds were against you growing up at all, especially of surviving your first year, let alone the next ten. Consider what the odds were that you would have been a serf, or a slave for at least some portion of your life (more likely were you female), even if not born into that condition, whether as a war captive or acquired by those ubiquitous slave traders, some of whom you might call Vikings. Consider what it meant to be poor and that you had to hand either yourself or your children over to your creditor or his assignee to serve as a debt slave when your crop failed and you could not repay the loan you had taken out to purchase seed corn the year before. You needed the loan to buy the seed to plant because you had eaten up the bushels you had set aside from the previous fall's meager harvest for the next spring's sowing, but by February you and your family were starving before your eyes. What could you do except postpone the reckoning? And hope.

3

Competition

LET'S START IN PARADISE in the Garden of Eden at the very beginning of humanity and 'historical' time.[1] It is elementary economics that scarcity generates value. Were a resource available at zero cost, like food in the Garden of Eden, it would have no value beyond its immediate use value. That explains the Fall, does it not? The only thing that had value in Eden was the one scarce item, made scarce by the prohibition that attached to it, the fruit of the forbidden tree. No wonder Eve ate of it. That was the only thing in the garden *worth* anything. It matters not whether we say it was desire that made it valuable or value that made it desirable, though really it is the latter. If we assume, like most commentators, that the Fall took place very quickly, probably early on the first day,[2] we do not have to worry about those small twinges of desire to eat, though the time twixt desire and its satisfaction would be very short, so desire would not be much more than a minimal drive, and not experienced as it often is among us as torment. Desire itself is at war with the idea of Paradise, it being impossible to imagine Paradise with or without it.

For millennia commentators, who invariably happened to be men, have blamed Eve, imbuing her with post-Lapsarian failures and shortcomings—vanity, irrationality, contrariness, weakness of will—in effect denying her any other motive than one that would allow men to say as they shook their heads disapprovingly, "wouldn't ya know it was a woman who screwed it all up?" We can be fairer: if in Eden there cannot be competition for wealth or possessions because there is no scarcity, there still can be positional competition, between Adam and Eve, and with God, that is, who gets to give orders and be looked up to. The snake, no dummy, is playing off her quest for knowledge, a competition academics like myself know well but that God has denied to her and her mate. Who with an ounce of fellow feeling could blame her, and that without any desire to curry favor with feminists or heel to the demands of political correctness? The only reason we can give that would have her disobey God's command before Adam eventually would have anyway is either that she is smarter or that she must play second fiddle to him and resents it, or both: "So when the woman saw . . . that the tree was to be desired to make one wise, she took of its fruit and ate."

Moreover, Eve (and Adam) in plentiful Eden cannot rationally understand the threat that backs the command not to eat of that tree. She cannot contemplate what a future of scarcity might hold, because she is without the knowledge to make that calculation, the knowledge having been denied both to her and Adam and only available to one who eats the forbidden fruit. The loss of Eden can only be valued *after* it has been taken away. Eve cannot be accused of irrationality, at least in some strict sense of rationality, since the costs and benefits as yet had no prices available to put into the rationality equation. That would require knowledge from which she was by divine command excluded. But the violation of the taboo created a world of scarcity in which now myriad different things have value.

Temptation did not come from any inherent value in the fruit, and even if, as I supposed, there was some vague desire for knowledge of good and evil, neither of those concepts could have any sense yet. The desire to eat the forbidden fruit was really a function of the NO that had been pasted on the tree. The NO generated the desire. A three-year-old knows that NO means it is likely that delectable or fun things are being denied, more often than merely dangerous things, and dangerous things are often sources of excitement and thrills, so the desirable lurks in them too. Even your dog knows that NO denies the desirable; otherwise, you would not be barking NO at her to get away from that rotting squirrel corpse or the human food on the table. Even should you discover that what was prohibited was not all you imagined it might be, the very violation of the prohibition is often a pleasure in itself, an act of primal freedom.

So now we have scarcity. Actually, it was there in some respect even before creation, for Chaos is depicted as a constant battle in which the primordial waters battle other forms of goop for dominance. The ancient myths could no more imagine that the time before time began as a quiet empty state of nothingness in which something was not struggling against something else for dominance than it is possible for me to imagine any human encounter, like a handshake or a kiss or inviting people over for dinner, without having some competitive aspect to it. Why? Because we grade and rank and compare the performances and there is always the risk of failure and thus of mortification, or at a minimum some embarrassment, in the simplest and most trivial of interactions.

For starters, let me set forth a strong position: it is impossible to escape certain bounded competitions, no matter how hard you try to avoid them, even if you go off to a desert island and live in a society of one. A Stoic, a Buddhist, or a saint will reject certain forms of competitiveness, especially those that are the essential markers of classic honor cultures whose demands and vanities they wish to escape. But are these vanities all escapable? Though, as a programmatic statement, the Stoic and the Buddhist will insist that they have turned their back on vain competition, on the passions that motivate it, they readily admit it is not easy to do so. They know it takes training, a real commitment to discipline, unless one were lucky enough to have been born without passions or desires. We cannot just wish competitiveness away, unless you want to eliminate every form of scarcity imaginable. And the pursuit of a difficult goal for self-improvement brings scarcity along for the ride, because it is so hard to achieve. Few manage it; most fail. The training to free yourself of competitiveness is a detox regimen some would say involves no less competitiveness than when you cared for worldly vanities like honor and wealth, for as you know there is honor, praise, and esteem in being known as Cato the Younger, or in having achieved Nirvana. In no way do I mean to undermine the strength of character that such types manifest, but they cannot escape certain ironies that accompany their pursuit. That is the broad claim; examples and hopefully some nuance follow.

Start with elementary basics: with scarcity comes competition for the scarce resource. Humans and other animals compete with members of their own species and against other species for access to food and space. In a sense, space is food at one remove, providing the ground and access to water for things to grow, and the territory from which you can claim the right to exclude competitors for game. This competition, as is only too obvious, provides a common cause for war, or within communities, for feud and dispute, and it demands rules of regulation we can call law that channel the competition into less costly forms.[3] Either we bear the costs of fighting others for access to what they claim as their territory or we have to bear the costs of fences, and defenses, and of a legal system to protect against their acquisitive and thus competitive designs on our territory. This is all rather trite, and it passes over myriad qualifications and complications, but it will do for an introduction.

That is one kind of competition. Call it loosely and inadequately distributional competition. It can be mostly, but not completely, distinguished from what are called competitions for positional goods, which also are a function of a scarcity much severer in some sense than competition for food, land, and control of natural resources. The standard positional good involves rank ordering. There can be only one Premier League winner, one gold medalist, one most valuable player, one king, one president. There are some qualified exceptions that allow for splitting up a rank for sharing, working reasonably well when Diocletian established the tetrarchy, and less well in medieval Norway where shared kingship in the eleventh and especially twelfth centuries led to incessant civil war. In some domains, the scarcity of positional goods is softened by the position having an expiration date; you are the champion for this year, for this Olympiad, or for the next Tour de France. Once your term is up you will then join a prestigious club of restricted membership of former gold medalists and champions, among whom you will also be ranked, and the honor of being in that club can be lost entirely: ask Lance Armstrong or, for that matter, someone who fails to live up to the status of once having been a champ should he become, say, a child molester or murderer. Kings? They ordinarily hold their rank as long as they live, hoping they outlast the pool of likely assassins among which figure prominently uncles, brothers, cousins, nephews, wives, and sons, though sons usually outsource killing dad, as dad does too when his dear son, now age twenty-one, cannot disguise his impatience at dad's continuing to live when he is ready to inherit the realm.

But once dead the competition is not over, for dead kings are ranked against their predecessors and successors as to who was the best or worst of them.

Though positional goods represent the ranking in a closed system, it may be possible to pump a kind of feel-good asset into the system to make all those in the game feel better about themselves even though their position relative to others in the game stays the same. Take, for instance, Japanese soldiers in World War II, where the performance of some 90% of the soldiery was death before dishonor. It had to be demoralizing to be playing in a league that good. The utterly average Japanese soldier would qualify for a Victoria Cross, or a US Medal of Honor, or even a German Pour le Mérite. In his own world, he was just a guy. The only direction that a Japanese soldier could go was down, the ultimate sacrifice being merely the common baseline, the starting point. Setting the average that incredibly high makes the culture less properly an honor culture than a culture of pure shame, if such a distinction makes any sense.[4] In one you seek to rise; in the other you put all your effort into not falling. Imagine, though, a unit of Japanese soldiers facing a unit of Americans or Brits, or Russians in 1904–5; don't those merely average Japanese soldiers all feel pretty good about themselves relative to their enemy, knowing that they play in a more demanding league, the competition stiffer, more rigorous? You might hear them say, or certainly they would think: hell, our worst guy is better than their best, so even the below-average Japanese guys get to feel like something less than losers, for they become the purest emblem of Japanese superiority. Thus is the pie of their system expanded somewhat by comparison with other whole systems, but do not think we have thereby violated the law of conservation of good things, for this Japanese enlargement of pride comes at the expense of Americans, Brits, Russians, Chinese, and so on. Recall those happy Danes who get part of their satisfaction and self-satisfaction from knowing that they are not Hungarians or, for that matter, Americans.

The Norse unabashedly delighted in ranking people and had a party game called a *mannjafnaðr*, literally a man-ranking, man-comparing game. People would sit around and propose who the first, second, and third most honorable man or woman in the district or in the room was.

It could get ugly; hurt feelings in an old-fashioned honor society could cut deep. Reports one saga:

> There was a lot of ale drinking. They spoke of 'man-comparing,' who was the greatest man in the district, the foremost chieftain. And there was no agreement, as is often the case when there is a man-comparing. Most went with Snorri goði as the greatest, but some named Arnkel. There were even some who named Styr.[5]

Snorri's response was to have Arnkel killed. Yet another saga mentions a *mannjafnaðr* in which Erlend claimed no one to be as brave as Kalf, while Illugi claimed that that prize belonged to Thorgrim. "The tale ended this way: Erlend killed Illugi for no other reason than that."[6]

The competition for positional goods makes for good stories. Seating arrangements are a case in point, one of the chief generators of strife ever since people began eating together. Seating places, whether on mats or stones or chairs, from thrones to dunce stools, are famously ranked and graded by where they are situated and who has the right, or earns the right, to sit in a particular place. The nightmarish, most hauntingly truthful childhood game about scarcity and its anxieties is what we called musical chairs. Do you not remember how you felt playing it when just seven years old? The chairs get ever scarcer with each stop of the music, and so do the human children competing to sit on them, the one left standing each time the music stops deemed a loser. There is always one less chair than there are kids, and the odds of surviving each round get progressively worse. The game starts out mostly as a competition for resources—our distributional competition—but once the last chair goes to one of the final two competitors, then it is about winning the prized positional good.

I published a book on *Njáls saga* a few years ago. That is the best saga in a tough competition for the best of the sagas. Though start points of a blood feud are always matters for reassessment and reinterpretation as the feud goes on, the start point in *Njáls saga* is pretty clear: it is about who gets to sit where at a feast. The feud ends some twenty-five years later after both sides have largely destroyed each other.

Enter an Icelandic farmhouse of a wealthy farmer hosting a feast. On each side of the long fire down the center of the hall are benches set along the walls. There are thus two seats of honor one in the middle of each side, with the seats ranked on each side downward the farther they are from the center. On one side sits the host and his crew, the host determining the arrangement and taking the seat of honor or giving it up for the occasion to one he wishes to honor. In many instances, as at your family's dinner table, it is understood that certain people have their seat. On the other side are arrayed the guests and their crew. It is not always clear who does the arranging for the guests. Sometimes the leader of the guests' entourage, say, the head of the bride's family if this is a wedding feast, will array his group, assuming a task that is too risky for the host to undertake, for he might not know the pecking order in that family. On the dais at one end of the long benches, the women of rank are seated, and here too the center seat is the seat of honor, and there is only one.

Because of their close friendship, Gunnar and Njal used to take turns at inviting one another to an autumn feast. This time it was Gunnar's turn to attend Njal's feast and so he and Hallgerd [Gunnar's wife] went to [Njal's farm].

Njal gave them a warm welcome. Helgi [Njalsson] and his wife Thorhalla were out when they arrived, but returned after a little while. Bergthora [Njal's wife] went over to the dais with Thorhalla and said to Hallgerd, "Move down for this woman."

Hallgerd said, "I'm not moving down for anyone, like some outcast hag."

"I am in charge here," said Bergthora; and Thorhalla took her seat. (ch. 35)

That is the beginning. Thorhalla lives in the home of her father-in-law, Njal, with her husband, Njal's son Helgi, and the seat Hallgerd takes is Thorhalla's every day. She married down into Njal's family and that family continues to recognize her high standing by conferring on her the woman's seat of honor. Hallgerd is the wife of the warrior hero Gunnar and of high social standing herself; she is also a guest. Thorhalla is not present when Hallgerd arrives, so Hallgerd either unthinkingly, or aggressively, or even justifiably assumes the seat to be hers by the rules of hospitality and her own social rank. The hostess has other ideas.

There seem to be so many ways to have resolved this awkward situation fairly easily. Bergthora, the hostess, could have refused to make such a big deal of it; Thorhalla could have said, "Oh that's okay, Hallgerd is welcome to sit there"; and Hallgerd could have said, "Oh I'm sorry, I thought Thorhalla was visiting elsewhere." No one takes this tack. Why? The seat matters too much, there is only one, and it is thus very scarce, and aggressive competition for honor is no less female than male. I might add that an uncle of mine, the husband of my father's sister, never forgave my mother for where he was seated at my sister's wedding. Many readers will have similar family stories.[7]

We cannot just blame competitiveness as some evil that would make the world nicer if it would go away or be disallowed. The blame cannot rest on competition itself. Where was the graciousness here that could have resolved the dispute? Is not graciousness something that can be competed for too, the reputation for being the most gracious hostess, the most generous host? Would it not be a good thing for people to compete for the honor of being most gracious? You cannot say that graciousness is by definition not competitive, because you would be dead wrong if you did. Anytime there is a virtue, you will gain status or praise or honor if you have the reputation for having that virtue; there will be rankings and competitions and they cannot be avoided, for people will compare.

Reconsider our law of conservation of good things from the last chapter, to which we must add a wrinkle. Competition for graciousness will produce more graciousness, though it might be a bit cheaper in a small parody of the justificatory commonplace about the benefits to the consumer that flow from competition in a capitalist system, where competition will ideally force the price of goods down to as low as they can go and still retain the same quality. But in virtue competitions, cheaper has a different relation with constant quality, for some of the graciousness will be hypocritical, a show for appearance's sake and lacking the ideal gracious motive. Some competitions are easier to determine who ranks where, like which seat is yours or who won the football game, but when people are discussing virtue and who is the most virtuous, they will be engaged in a ranking game, as pure a competition as there is but much harder to score, for inner states and motives are hard to get at, and exactly what counts as a plus or a minus will be more open to dispute. Virtue competitions invite hypocrisy to attend, yet that not need be a bad thing. To pass as gracious, for instance, one will actually have to behave better than Bergthora did. The quality of the deeds will improve even if the motives are not always perfect. This is the compact and brilliant insight of La Rochefoucauld's "Hypocrisy is the homage vice pays to virtue" (Maxim 218).

Will a round table solve the seating arrangement competition? One of the earliest stories children are treated to, even in the United States, is the tale of King Arthur's wisdom in solving this prime bone of contention. But making a table round will not prevent assigning ranked values to the seats. We can predict that some will automatically be lower-status seats, and that only three will immediately qualify for higher status, not including Arthur's (and there will be very little disagreement as to which ones they are): the ones on Arthur's immediate right and left and the one at six o'clock right across from him.

How about not competing, even accepting or welcoming defeat, which is one way to understand turning the other cheek, but manifestly not the way St. Paul understood it. Waiving a claim can be a winning move in a competition of who gets to look down on whom. As Paul says in Romans (12.20): forgiving your enemy is like pouring hot coals on his head; forgiveness, as he sees it, is fighting fire with fire. Consider this scene, which gets played out in reality more than one would think. I have even witnessed a fight in high school that took this style. Imagine, say, in late seventeenth-century England or America, the bumptious town bully punching a Quaker, who takes each shot without a flinch, does not go down, and stares back, maybe even intoning an "I forgive you," maybe not. The audience, if not already by blow two, but surely by number three, is hooting at the bully and pulls him away. The Quaker has just won the conventional tough-man competition, and also won his own Quaker virtue competition against the violently competitive world his sect rejects. In effect, two games are being played at once. The Quaker wins both the aggressive and the passive game.[8] Will he be able to deny himself a feeling of triumphalism?

There are negative competitions too; these are usually imposed on others by gossip, as in who is the biggest loser, but sometimes by the law too, or by specially named seats. We think of these competitions as shaming devices, and we should not be surprised that competition for honor should also be mirrored by a competition of shame avoidance, on not being branded the worst; the most cowardly; the fattest, ugliest, shortest, weakest, stupidest; the one entitled to the dunce stool or electric chair. People also speak of negative lotteries. These figure in more than a few memoires of the death camps and Gulag. Where to stand in line *not* to get selected, *not* to get picked, is the name of the game. Losing the lottery is winning it in that upside-down world.

So competitive are we, so given to ranking things and competing for honor, that even badges of dishonor have ways of becoming a currency of honor. In my high school we were punished by having days of detention, which meant staying after school in a room with a tough teacher to guard us. Pretty soon there was a race to see who could get the most detention for misbehaving. We also noted that there was a limit to how long we could be interned—until the last day of school—and then all misbehavior would be for free. And the person who got the most detention the soonest? Why, what a guy, the baddest of all.

Another small wrinkle: the very contest for esteem, for honor, almost necessarily generates a parallel anti-honor discourse. Thersites in the *Iliad* is the classic example, but for all we know Thersites is only ridiculing one kind of honor game, the game the big guys play, but back in the camp, presumably, there are rankings that Thersites cares to do well in, like storytelling, being funny, or who can get Odysseus the angriest. When Odysseus soundly beats him to a pulp for being ugly, contemptible, and disrespectful, we see Thersites winning the anti-honor competition, whether he wants to enter that competition or not, though differently from the straight-out honor won by the kid in my high school who was 'punished' with the most detention after school.

There is no escaping the competitiveness of honor groups, for competitiveness is inherent in their make-up. By honor groups I mean to indicate any group in which people are in the same boat so to speak, roughly equal, whether as colleagues, family members, historians, welders, electricians, crime fiction writers, tennis players, and so on. I do not mean that they have to be classic heroic honor societies. Sewing clubs, reading groups, fashion shows, and prayer meetings all qualify, for some or all the members will have a jealous eye as to where their performance stands relative to the other members. There will of course be attempts to escape the unavoidable determinations of rank. One can quit the honor group and its particular game, though that group will for a length of time continue to count you a loser among them for quitting. You will be a virtual member, like it or not. You might even go down in the group's unofficial history as the biggest creep ever to have been a member.

If you achieve Nirvana or, in the Stoic world, if you can match Cato the Younger, you have made it; you have attained full control of those passions that would prompt most people to desire, if not always to seek, acclaim, glory, or wealth.

Easier fixes than the rigorous disciplines of Buddhism and Stoicism, or of strict asceticism, have been offered up to dampen the passions that fuel the competition for acclaim. They are fairly easy to mock, like those regimes of enforced noncompetitiveness where the prize goes to the one who can be least competitive, but everyone or no one will get it. For example, compare the Danish law of Jante, where no one is to rise above others in the interests of communal equality, and the American version where every person, no matter how inept, is declared special and his own type of genius. In one culture, no one wins the MVP award; in the other everyone does. Do you think the kids do not know whom they would pick first or second if they had to choose sides for a football game or a math contest?

What pretenses and self-deceptions must we engage in to deny we are competing when people, including ourselves, might well suspect we are fighting hard to look good in the game at hand? What if the very thing being valued is not to care where you stand, that that very caring is the deadly sin of pride? When humility, as in Christianity, is made one of the chief virtues of your system, how do you prevent a humility contest from arising, and prevent growing big headed if you should win it? The early church fathers were on to this, and so was that most wonderfully strange of authors Sir Thomas Browne in the seventeenth century: "Diogenes I hold to be the most vain-glorious man of his time, and more ambitious in refusing all Honours, than Alexander in rejecting none."[9] But the classic statement of the Catch-22 comes from the *Autobiography of Benjamin Franklin*, a man of genius, one of several my country was once blessed to have steering it at a key moment in its history.

Franklin decided he would, as an exercise in self-improvement, keep a diary of his daily exercise of virtue. He made a list of twelve virtues, intending to note instances of improvement or backsliding in each of them regularly. He showed it to a Quaker friend, who told him that humility was missing from his list and that since many thought him a rather prideful and arrogant man, shouldn't he better include it and work to subdue this particular failing of his? Franklin says this:

> I cannot boast of much success in acquiring the *reality* of this virtue [humility], but I had a good deal with regard to the *appearance* of it. I made it a rule to forbear all direct contradiction to the sentiments of others, and all positive assertion of my own. . . . I soon found the advantage of this change in my manner; the conversations I engag'd in went on more pleasantly. The modest way in which I propos'd my opinions procur'd them a readier reception and less contradiction.

In short, his fake humility got him everything he wanted. He discovered that the mere appearance of humility worked better than his more aggressive styles at gaining his goal. There is even the roguish implication that the fake version worked better than real humility would have. That he pulled off this manipulative con tickled him to no end. He concludes:

> In reality, there is, perhaps, no one of our natural passions so hard to subdue as *pride*. Disguise it, struggle with it, beat it down, stifle it, mortify it as much as one pleases, it is still alive, and will every now and then peep out and show itself; . . . for, even if I could conceive that I had compleatly overcome it, I should probably be proud of my humility.[10]

Most medievalists and people who study religion have some familiarity with holiness contests,[11] whose most frequent coin in pre-Reformation Christianity was self-mortification. One renounced worldly vanities. Early to go were sex, wealth, and food. Fasting quickly turned competitive. How could it not? People kept raising the bar and the stakes, literally raising poles to sit on, nibbling very modest amounts of nearly inedible food hoisted up to provide just enough not to starve to death. In Ireland you might see who could stand the longest in cold water while reciting the entire Book of Psalms. Hair shirts became almost mandatory. One had a hard time not being proud of his or her oozing sores, until we get to St. Catherine of Siena, who really jacked up the stakes: she drank up the pus of a sick nun's infected breast. Match that. I am humbler and holier than you could ever think of being, the best of all self-mortifiers.

One can see the elaborate devotions to the wounds of Christ as an almost blasphemous contest to see if you could match his suffering, you reproducing in yourself the Man of Sorrows, which you knew was an imitation (the valued goal of *imitatio Christi*), and sometimes so good a copy that you miraculously generated stigmata. I do not mean to suggest that the people engaging in these practices were impiously motivated. They were motivated primarily by a desire for holiness and worshipfulness as they understood it. But the competitive side cannot be eliminated. Imagine the sense of failure in those devotees of the holy wounds who were not blessed with stigmata. People would set to ranking the performers, just as the guardians of saints' relics would have their saint compete for miracles with other saints, and people voted with their feet by visiting the shrines where the word was out that that saint had performed more cures than other saints for hundreds of miles around.

We cannot ignore Jesus's hostility to certain manifestations of holiness competition. He could not bear people giving alms competitively (or fasting ostentatiously). He calls them hypocrites and recommends giving alms in secret and pretending not to fast while fasting (Matt. 6.1–18). The poor would probably much prefer that Jesus leave matters alone when it came to competitive almsgiving. They might not unreasonably think they were better off having to fight each other for the gold and silver flung about ostentatiously by those givers trying to outdo each other in publicly played generosity contests, announced by trumpets, than they would be if alms-giving were done privately. Jesus does not like the motive of those noisy givers: public acclaim. Yet Jesus makes sure to inform the secret giver that he is still playing before an audience—actually a bigger one, the Father who will reward him in heaven. What does the knowledge of that mega-reward do to the unostentatious giver's motives? As I suggested with St. Paul and the tough

Quaker, the issue is more a fight about styles than a fight about motives. There is still a game being played in which people are ranked, one more noisy, the other quieter.

Jesus is setting up a new game in which people are judged and ranked, passive death and martyrdom revalued as glorious triumph. Honor is still there, the game is still there, but the way points are scored and what counts as a goal or a touchdown have changed. If the first shall now be last and the last first, we still have our ranking game played with a vengeance, and not even veneered by denial. Jesus seriously wants out of the classic macho honor game, but it is impossible to do so without establishing a new honor game, less overtly macho perhaps, but it too soon develops its own brand of machismo as a contest pitting patient sufferers against each other, the martyr who can take the most torture.

Return to the Stoic or Buddhist, or a self-mortifying monk or holy hermit, all of whom mean to turn their backs on the vanities of the world and its competitions for wealth, honor, and power. Can we assume he does not care what others think of him? We can concede that he does not care what those worldly others for whom he has genuine contempt think of him, but what of those who, like himself, have chosen similar paths to holiness, and whom he respects, whom he might even worship? Suppose he really does put what these respected others think on the back burner of his consciousness, though to do so is not so easy. As we noted, it is likely to take serious discipline, the ability to sustain a difficult commitment over a long period of time. You need to have the inner resources to stick to the regimen when your still imperfectly trained self starts weakening, and you start sneaking a peek to see if those respected others count you as one of them, or even maybe as having surpassed them.[12] And should you take to the woods or a mountaintop or a desert to get away from them, to make it impossible to see or hear what they think or where you stand among them, then how do you blind yourself to the judgment of your own inner audience?

How do you not compete with or against prior or future versions or visions of yourself? Part of the training regimen would involve you measuring yourself against yourself, keeping score, no differently from a four-hundred-meter sprinter tracking his performances when training, not against others, but against himself and the stopwatch, to mark if he is training properly and successfully. Are you able to repress the chagrin and disappointment at backward steps in your regimen? Are you able to avoid self-congratulation or, if not that, then some twinge of satisfaction in your progress? Does not striving for a goal, even if the goal is to free oneself of all passions that disturb virtue, need a certain kind of competitive spirit to carry it off, even if it is against other versions of yourself that you are competing? Are we not back in some weaker sense to Franklin's problem with humility, and the pride he fears would accompany his achieving it, were it possible for him to do so?

My fear is that so fallen is my soul that I am without the capacity to imagine a psychological state that true human saints must have reached. But let us look down lower, to people we might actually have met. Most of us know some truly humble people, or at least they are so good at faking it that we imagine their inner life is in accord with the external manifestations of the virtue. The performance is too good in certain unfakeable ways to be fake. It is perhaps not a mystery at all. Sure, they know and even care where they stand. They just handle it with grace, and as long as they are doing okay in some reasonably objective sense, they are at ease. That does not prevent them from wanting to do their tasks well; it is rather that when they succeed at a task, that is, in itself, sufficient satisfaction. But isn't that a kind of pride? How does he know that he has done well without engaging in comparison and judging against others' performances or against his own? Yet, so what if his satisfaction shares some DNA with pride? It is more about not making people suffer your superiority if you have it or imposing on them your inferiority if that is where you stand. I guess. Is there no risk in becoming too complacent in your virtue that in fact it has become too easy, making no demands on you at all? But then again, what is wrong with that; that is not easy virtue in the bad sense, is it? Isn't one of the goals of moral training to make it easy to do the right thing? But then won't there be some kind of competition over for whom it is easier? I am all tied up in knots.

Let's elevate our account. Suppose, moved by the lives of the desert fathers, you seek for yourself a life of prayer and self-mortification. For that purpose you move to a small island in the fens of East Anglia, like St. Guthlac (d. 715), to avoid the world. Will you be able to suppress that you are following a script, not of your own making, that places you in a group of those who are, if not quite seeking, then making themselves eligible, not unknowingly, for sainthood? How can you repress that you may be impressing people with your ability to reject earthly honor, especially since you have given up wealth and position to seek your solitude? Was it not, in part, your own being impressed with others who sought such holy loneliness that suggested it to you? Soon you find that people are seeking you out, asking you to heal them. You will be told that your holiness works better than some other hermit who is living in a cleft of a crag somewhere in the Hebrides. Guthlac thought his island near inaccessible, but a lot of people, important people, beat a path to him.

Since others will not leave you alone, knowledge of the standings of the league you are playing in will, unless you are utterly obtuse, be part of the devilish temptations you must deal with. On that score, let's end this discussion with how smart some early medieval abbot was about the Franklin problem in a world of competitive humility, though the real miracle we are about to hear is not the one performed by the young monk, but that of the abbot's psychological acuity. The story comes from Gregory of Tours writing in the sixth century. It deals with a truly humble person, and a desperate effort to keep him that way against the very processes I have been discussing.

A boy wishes to be accepted into a monastery. The abbot tries to discourage him, telling him how rigorous the discipline is, and he so young. The boy promised that with God's help he would do his best and so he was admitted. He turned out to be humble and God fearing in all that he did. One sunny day the brothers carted out grain to dry in the sun and they left the young monk to watch over the grain. Suddenly a storm came up. The youth did not know what to do. The brothers were too far away to call for help; there was too much grain to think of carting it back to the barn in time. So he threw himself face down and prayed, asking God to spare the grain from rain. And lo, the cloud split, says Gregory, "if what I have heard is true" and passed on each side of the grain, not a kernel getting wet. In the meantime, the other monks and the abbot had come running to save the grain and they saw what was happening. The young monk, still face down praying, was without knowledge of the miracle in progress:

When the abbot saw what had happened, he lay down in prayer be-side the [young] monk. When the rain had completely passed over he told the youth to get up and ordered him to be seized and beaten. "It is for you, my son, he said, to grow more and more humble in the fear and service of God, not to puff yourself up with prodigies and miracles." He had him shut in his cell for a whole week and made him fast in expiation to prevent him from becoming too pleased with himself and so that he might learn to mend his ways. (4.34)

Gregory says that he has heard from reliable sources that the monk remained abstinent, a rigorous faster, until this day, even if Gregory had some small doubts—"if what I have heard is true"—about the miracle of the parting cloud. He introduced the story thus: "I will now tell something which happened in another monastery. I do not propose to give the name of the monk concerned, for he is still alive and if he should read what I have written he might be filled with vainglory and so lose virtue." Gregory is merely assuming in that brief phrase all that I have taken this entire chapter to say.

The abbot in Gregory's tale could have written my piece. He is con-cerned with precisely the issues I have been raising. He knows the miracle-working powers of this simple pure soul depend on his being simple and pure, and it is next to impossible for him now not to swell with pride, or become self-conscious that swelling with pride is a risk for him. People will make it next to impossible for him to maintain his humility, as Gregory notes. Stories and sagas will be told of him, even in his own lifetime. People will seek him out. He has won; he is in first place in a competition he did not know he was in but that others will place him in anyway, and the competition, or the self-consciousness of it, might well cause him to lose first place and fall out of the game.

4

Vile Jelly

SOME OF THE INVITATIONS that my disgust book elicited would be too disgusting to mention. I would remind my inviters before refusing that to have written *The Anatomy of Disgust,* one had to be plagued by fastidiousness and somewhat horrified by human embodiment.[1] This chapter revisits themes in my disgust book. I had been unwilling to face the subject again since that book appeared in 1997, having said then what I had to say on the topic.[2] That book must bear some blame for spawning an algae bloom of articles and books on the topic. I add some fresh pink and plump excrescences here.

After puberty, there is very little about human embodiment that isn't at the core of what we find disgusting, except when overcome by 'love' or alcohol. Fingernails, for instance, don't work, hard and dry though they may be, but when you knew someone who saved all his finger and toe-nail clippings in a jar, they too partnered with the softer and squishier and hairier stuff to elicit disgust quite readily. Even tears are only fragilely on the side of disembodied angels. They must be prompted by sorrow or joy, and not too copious in their flow, for then the nose starts to run, compromising the purity of those tears with mucus. Tears have no privilege at all if they are induced by an eye infection; nor are they granted purity if prompted by fear. Cowardice makes them shameful, unless they appear in a small child fighting bravely with all her might to hold them back.

Even the eyes, the symbol of sentient beauty, the windows to our souls—though we share them with squid and reptiles, even scallops, none of which are supposed to have souls—those eyes are nothing but "vile jelly" in the Duke of Cornwall's appalling, though inspired, image he affixes to the second of Gloucester's eyes as he gouges it out of the old man's head. He addresses the unattached eyeball directly and familiarly, "Where is *thy* luster now?" (*King Lear* 3.7.86). Gloucester, eyeless, is not worth the words.

Violently extracting eyes is the bread and butter of a medievalist such as I, it being the signatured way of putting an opponent out of the game in the political world of Byzantium, borrowed with avidity by the Carolingians and ninth-century Bulgarians and applied with zeal by fathers to sons right in the Carolingian heartlands. Thus, Charles the Bald had his son Carloman blinded, after the humiliation of tonsuring him did not make the young man any more willing to please his father (873 CE).[3]

One might play on words and say that so much of disgust is a matter of taste, taste in the sense of the actual experience of evaluating one's attraction to or revulsion for food. But I have argued that the focus on the sense of taste in much of the earlier psychological research on disgust was suggested by the philological accident of the rise of the word *degoût* in French, transported to English as *disgust*, where what we call disgust was previously denoted by other more general words. In Middle English it was indicated by the words *abhorrence* and *irksomeness*; in the Romance languages by reflexes of Latin *fastidium*, *fastidious* ending up in English to mean its near opposite, describing someone very keen to avoid anything remotely disgusting and who risks thereby becoming disgustingly prissy.

Lately disgust has been claimed as an evolutionary response to disease avoidance.[4] I am unconvinced. Can it be that off-putting ugliness or foul tastes or bad smells save us from more disease and death than we are blissfully led to by the allure of nightshade beauty or by the various incarnations of Melusine? Poisons hardly advertise their lethality by tasting or smelling bad; they too can adapt. More conservation of good things (see chapter 2)? Think too of the wonderful cheeses and lutefisk that these scientists of disgust fail to account for. And then why too are so many foods—pizzas, quiches, thick tasty stews—unable to disguise their uncanny resemblance to vomit? These evolutionary psychologists do try one's patience sometimes, and one need not be a Bible-thumping creationist to feel the genetically determined desire to roll one's eyes in contempt; their functionalism misses just what is so uncannily enchanting, psychologically and sociologically, about the disgusting.

Our diction for taste and smell is quite limited: "tastes good" or "smells bad" is more than half of it. Think how irritating it is for most people to listen to the descriptions of wines and whiskies, how pretentious it all sounds. The English vocabulary of disgust is mostly one of tactility, which tracks what we think of as ugliness when perceived visually: thus the slimy, clammy, squishy, greasy, suppurating, viscous, oozing, festering, squiggly, wriggling, and scummy. Disgust is revulsion with the look and feel of many of life's necessary and inevitable processes, which, of course, include death, sickness, and decay, a fat weed rooted on Lethe's wharf. Life is polluting. What is the worst temperature a public toilet seat can have? 37°C, 98.6°F.

The fact is, your ennobling human dignity aside, you are very much like a pond clothed in algae scum, forever generating, rotting, and regenerating. We are squishy and slimy on the inside at our best, and often crusty and pimply on the outside, when not at our best. There is nothing quite like skin gone bad, the curse of old age, and of adolescence too; even skin at its infantile best is often blighted by diaper rash. Skin also comes with fairly large holes in it, often lined by mucous membranes. The holes let the outside in and the inside out; they emit, leak, and admit. They are danger zones, vulnerable, and defended not only by disgust but also by real laws that can get you imprisoned and by myriad religious rituals and prohibitions that can get you damned or cursed if you breach them. But the defenses are never quite up to the job, weakened as they are at times by love and at times by sheer rebellion against rules disallowing playing in the dirt. Then there is infancy, before the rules of disgust have been rammed into the brain, and old age, where one just gives up adhering to them in the face of demoralization and sensory dullness.

What is so appallingly perfect about Gloucester's eyes being figured as vile jelly, thus suggesting supping on them, is also that jelly, as good as it might be as aspic or as the quintessence of fruit we put on bread or in pastries, makes us recoil in its more natural pre-culinary forms—snail slime, the very substance of worms, slugs, leeches, raw liver, even a pumping heart or a jellyfish. Vile jelly captures the revulsion of exactly what we are made of better than most anything else, halfway between mucus and semen, the scum from which we come.

Disgust, more than any other emotion, is the one most keenly attuned to perception as perception, to the senses as senses, and though fear shares a concern to save the body, disgust is more nuanced: it cares to keep the *self*, not just the body but the soul too, free from contamination, mostly contamination by other human beings. You touch a slug or a salamander and you wash up, so too with dog excrement, but some random person sticks his tongue in your mouth in a show of desire not shared by you and it is not clear how you can purify yourself. Someone watching might see you contaminated forever, that being still the case in a good portion of the world, where the purity of women is obsessed upon in ways that are lethal to them. Your sense of taste or lack thereof in whom you privilege to be intimate with might make others think you lack more than judgment and taste, but that you are also polluted and thus polluting.

Disgust impinges on all sorts of values and involves all the senses except perhaps hearing, which operates mostly in the domain of annoyance and irritation on its aversive side. But annoyance can ooze over into disgust at times. Take certain styles of laughter, for instance. There are laughs—I am sure more than one or two of your colleagues have them—that are more than annoying; they can actually prompt homicidal thoughts in the sweetest of people. The timbre, the intrusiveness, its excessive frequency, independent of the actual content of what the person laughing finds funny, cancels that person as a fully moral being in some special sense of moral, a sense that makes us feel imperfectly moral ourselves for not being more tolerant. Are we disgusted by the laugh or the laugher? I think at times we cannot disaggregate them and condemn both.[5]

But not all intolerance is sending out false positives. Amazing, is it not, that what we deem to be "little things" are inevitably the biggest things in our lives, especially in our relations with others? A certain transient look can permanently mar an otherwise attractive face forever, and that transient look is as likely to be one of ecstasy as one of dull blankness or of anger or fear. Oh to escape the tyranny of little things that matter so much and curse us with a difficult, if not quite impossible, task of justifying our excessive response to them. But cosmic justice is done, for little things about you and me revolt others just as much as their little things revolt us; the only difference is that though we are hyperaware of the little things about them that revolt us, we are clueless as to what it might be about ourselves that revolts them. Mostly we just deny that we are revolting them: but of course we are. There are, however, those cursed moments when we have to see ourselves on film, in my case lecturing. I get ill when that happens. I once remarked to a student that I was unaware that I made so many faces when I talked, and it was mortifying to see myself thus. She said, "What? You mean you were unaware you make faces all the time? How is that possible?" That I am writing this sentence indicates I did not have cyanide readily available.

Life is a messy business, a process of flux and flow, growth and decay. It is very hard at times to keep a pious face and not smirk contemptuously when we speak of human dignity, supposedly an inalienable attribute of us all. We share rather more with tapeworms than with angels. For dignity compare your cat or the magnificent red-tailed hawk perched on a branch outside my office window as I type this, and for sweetness of spirit compare your dog.

Human bodies are problematic, except when they are packaged as baby flesh, the fat thighs of a four-month-old; a reprieve follows[6] and then come the horrors of puberty, when a surge of new hormones sometimes enable us to suppress the revulsion of hair in all the wrong places, new oozing emissions, new unpleasant smells. The hormones work to overcome disgust, disgust itself constituting a dare to overcome it, a challenge of sorts. Even in their prime there are only a small number of people whose nakedness does not elicit revulsion. Says Voltaire in his *Philosophical Dictionary*: "There are so few well-formed persons of both sexes, that nakedness might have inspired chastity, or rather disgust, instead of increasing desire."[7] Long before you get to my age the hormones cease to be produced in necessary quantities and the particular body parts they activated decay and breakdown. We are left with the self-loathing of contemplating our old body, its lack of tone, its nonresponsiveness to everything except pain, and above all its tactile and visual ugliness. All this is independent of whether or not we are fat.

The first disgust expression I observed on the faces of my children occurred roughly at three months, long before they could properly have the emotion disgust, which requires that mere aversion be suffused with ideas of defilement and contamination, coupled with a desperate concern to seek purification, often via ritual behaviors dedicated to that purpose. In each case, it was because they had a hair in their mouth. Now I ask you to imagine that you are eating at a restaurant and feel a hair in your mouth. You locate the hair and you pull, and it keeps coming and coming. The hair is a very long one. Isn't that, somewhat paradoxically, much more disgusting than if the hair were a mere half-inch long? If it is long it came from a head, still most likely a woman's head, the place where hair is charged with Eros. Its length bears the saving knowledge that it did not come from the pubic area or the armpits or, God forbid, from the back. What could be more reassuring than a long hair? Yet the longer the hair, the more consumed with disgust we are; it just keeps coming and coming. Again, it is not its taste but rather the feel of it. (The present fashion in men's beards as they head toward nineteenth-century length means that a long hair in the mouth has even more disgusting possibility now than it did when I first mused on the issue more than twenty years ago.)

You can see what it means to have disgust as one's topic: there are risks that come with the territory. For one: it risks disgusting the reader if one gets too particular or too suggestive. Two: disgust is linked almost inevitably to misanthropy, some of it mildly satirical and comical, some of it foul-spirited. Three: disgust makes it hard to be pious about sex and various attempts to link sex with human dignity; it ends up being the domain of toilet humor until puberty, and tasteless sex jokes thereafter. Last, but not least, it is impossible not to reveal too much about oneself, forcing an unintended spiritual autobiography—spiritual that suggests that spirit is but *flatus*. Yes, that is the Latin word that gives us *flatulence*.

The knowledge of how humans procreate does not come lightly to children. It should be clear already that such knowledge came especially hard to me. I managed to prevent the information from penetrating my consciousness until I was twelve. The boys with whom I was playing football one day mocked me when they found out I did not know; they delighted in informing me graphically, actually objectively, but to me it seemed horrifically excessive and crude. I had finally come to the age where I had no defenses against the sickening knowledge, having long known how puppies, kittens, calves, and piglets were produced. I burst into tears, something a twelve-year-old boy is never allowed to do for any reason whatsoever except for the death of the family dog. I blubbered tearfully: "My mom would never do anything like that." They were too tickled by my misery to find my tears disgusting.

If you have not already dismissed me as crazy, let me say, as I indicated earlier, that I believe it takes a person overly nice about the disgusting—it takes, in short, a fastidious person, deeply ambivalent about his and others' embodiment—to understand disgust: an Orwell, not some willfully transgressive sort, like Bataille or Genet, or some faux-hip academic or performance artist. It takes one who is ever fearful and vigilant that others are sources of contamination and defilement, but that is less than half of it: it is that *you* are as much a danger to yourself as others are to you. It is *you* who must deal with your own excrement every day, and only very rarely that you must deal with someone else's, usually your children's, where duty and love intervene. As I said in my disgust book, it is simply not true that our own excrement does not smell; the difference between my excrement and yours is that on occasion I can be proud of mine, or equally be disappointed by it; those sentiments are not available for another's excrement, again unless they are your babies or pets. Should either yours or my own find its way to my hand or onto my clothing, it would be difficult to apportion the degree of disgustingness between them. Mine is not much safer to me than yours would be.

I am not a psychologist, neuroscientist, or philosopher. My specialty is the world of the Icelandic sagas, mostly written in the thirteenth century, depicting a world of revenge, law, honor, and tough practicality, coupled with a consistent penchant for cold wit. I came to disgust, believe it or not, because of the sagas, where it figures virtually not at all. The sagas made me interested in the micro-politics of face-to-face encounters, of physical proximity to other humans, and of the fears and anxieties that obsess us when we reflect late at night upon the success or failure of simple routine encounters with others. One need not even wait until late at night; that sinking feeling can overwhelm one right *in medias res*, in the middle of a class or a lecture, or when reading page proofs of one's own thoughts and words, when it is too late to make serious changes.

If one never escapes anxiety about one's honor and its attendant fears of shame, one is, if properly socialized, acutely aware of the sentiments one reads on the faces and in the behaviors of others that signal disapproval, primarily when it is registered as disgust and contempt. Disgust and contempt were what the honorable person tried to avoid provoking in others; they were what shameful behavior would elicit in the eyes of others.[8]

So much of shame is experienced as disgust with oneself. Where would anything resembling self-consciousness be without disgust and shame; would the human self be possible, assuming it to exist, without these unpleasant emotions? Disgust governs our bodily orifices and motivates our efforts to keep them reasonably under control even when we are alone. Disgust governs our concern that we might smell, and this especially hits teenagers hard, and so too the lower classes, who end up dousing themselves in colognes and perfumes. Disgust, of course, governs sex and the love that sometimes may accompany it or be chased away by it.

Eating, like sex, is also fertile ground for disgust. Watching others stick food in their mouths, masticate it, shift it around with their tongues, and swallow can be a difficult experience. Some part of the reason that eating is one of the most densely ritualized activities in almost every culture is not only to forge community but also to keep the unseemliness of keeping our bodies nourished from undoing community—hence, at least among us, the importance of table manners, which one never quite succeeds in getting the nuances through to our kids, who no doubt are too much influenced by doing what you do, rather than what you say to do, probably with your mouth full. Luckily our attention is mostly focused on sating our own hunger and self-monitoring, with not that much time left over to watch others unless their manners are so bad as to intrude, variously by loud lip smacking, slurping, or burping. Notice too that eating is disgusting not because disgust is a matter of protecting the body from ingesting bad things as per the evolutionary psychologists, but because eating a ton of good and healthy things can be hard to watch. The thought of what chewing does to food is more than most can endure. It thus provides a perfect vehicle for the juvenile joke of showing your friends or siblings what you are eating by opening your mouth full of well-chewed food. And thus too the disgusting feel of this image from *Hamlet*: "he keeps them, like an ape, in the corner of his jaw; first mouthed, to be last swallowed" (4.2.16–17).

It is not a perverse intellectual exercise, but a scientific truth, to see the human animal as nothing more than a large feeding tube, a mouth at one end, an anus at the other.[9] We are a fancier version of those tube-like polyps with the cilia syphoning sea water through their bodies. The image of a human as a tube has generative power. The tubing runs for miles, from mouth to throat to stomach to intestines, small and large, and then departing the rectum, which is the last frontier where *you* reside, only to enter another tubing system constructed at taxpayer expense as we flush the toilet, and our food, once fit for kings, continues its journey down to a sunlit sea, where it becomes food for worms and undulating polyps. Some will discern that I am channeling—channels providing another image of tubing—Hamlet's melancholic musings on the egalitarianism of eating, excreting, and dying, the lot of kings as well as of beggars. We end up passing by a very circuitous route, unless given to cannibalism, where the route is as the crow flies, through each other's guts.

One of the features that distinguishes the embryology of roundworms and nematodes that eventually will eat us if we do not cheat them by cremation is that they develop their mouths before their anuses, whereas most of us 'higher forms' develop our anuses first, and the hole then slowly worms its way through the embryonic goo to end in making a mouth, completing the tube that is us, 'assholes' in origin and in essence.[10] The sense of ourselves as feeding tubes is hard to ignore in the rich West where food became so cheaply abundant that human fat became the marker of poverty rather than of wealth. It could be argued that the poor are fashion setters, by indirection. The rich look first to the poor to determine what *not* to look like themselves. When the poor were emaciated, the rich fattened themselves into *Stattlichkeit*, into portliness if male, plumpness if female. When the poor got fat the rich adopted ascetic regimes that could match an Irish monk. As a general matter beauty is what it means not to look poor.[11] There are some exceptions: some ancient, as when a few of the portly or plump rich were tempted to undertake self-mortifying religious devotions and starved themselves both to *be* and to *look* holy. Then there is the fantasy that informs the common fairytale motif that when a child of poor peasants grew up to be a beautiful woman or a handsome warrior, it turned out that they were foundlings of noble birth. One exception is recent: black inner-city boys set the standard for coolness for a lot of suburban white boys in the United States (it does not work quite as insistently for girls). But not for long. White kids adopting black styles grow up and grow out of their pathetic efforts to be the epitome of cool.

Then there is the horror of that aging body, which I mostly omit rather than repeat matters more fully developed in my *Losing It*. But I must tell of two visions that permanently scarred my retinas or led to the vitreous detachment that I endured a couple of years ago, generating random light shows for months. One occurred at the YMCA when my father took the ten-year-old me there. In the communal shower were several old men, some of whom were familiar to me from our synagogue, with their enormous stomachs hanging down over and mercifully completely obscuring their genitals. How was I ever to greet them or be greeted by them again? But that did not adequately prepare me for what I was to witness, without any foreknowledge or warning, when I, a naïve twenty-one-year-old puritanical American, first visited a beach in Europe and found Germans there of all ages, sizes, and shapes swimming naked, unembarrassed by their folds and sags, flaccidities and discolorations of flesh. I never recovered. There were, I suspect, more than a few of them who would have, or should have, prompted either envy or desire in me, depending on their sex, but the beautiful were sucked into invisibility by the overpowering gravitational force of ugliness.

So much of self-consciousness is tied up in self-evaluation. We range from narcissistic self-satisfaction to morbid self-loathing. But self-loathing and disgust eventually win the day, when we can no longer deny Hamlet's hostile words to Polonius about old men: "their faces are wrinkled, their eyes purging thick amber and plum-tree gum, and that they have a plentiful lack of wit, together with most weak hams" (2.2.198–99). John Lennon must have had these lines in mind when he sang of "yellow matter custard dripping from a dead dog's eye." Vile jelly yet again.

In medieval moral writing the disgusting was primarily imaged as the bodies of old men and old women, when not depicted as the hell of Satan's anus. Old age was an emblem to warn the carefree young that *et in Arcadia ego*, that they too would end up looking like the old people they mocked, yes mocked—much as in biblical times when stumbling blocks were set up to trip the blind and insults were shouted into the ears of the deaf, not merely the stuff of metaphor but of laugh-out-loud hijinks.

Being undesirable at any age is bad enough, but being inescapably undesirable after once, if lucky, having been desirable to some for one brief moment in time, or fancied oneself as having been, and though old, still believing that one is experiencing desire and fatuously still thinking oneself desirable, even if it was money that made you so, was unpardonable, as it still is today, Viagra, plastic surgery, Botox, liposuction, plastic hips, silicone breasts, lifted butts and eyelids notwithstanding. Only tons of money seems to provide a cure, not to pay for plastic surgery, but to buy 'friendship.'

An old man who married a young woman meant he deserved his cuckold horns for his presumption, and her disgust at his pathetic attempts at lovemaking was not always disguised. In Chaucer's *Merchant's Tale* the drollery of the understatement is priceless. Thus the fair young wife, May, after enduring a wedding night in bed with her ineffectual old husband:

> But God woot what that May thoughte in hir herte,
> Whan she hym saugh up sittynge in his sherte,
> In his nyght-cappe, and with his nekke lene;
> She preyseth nat his pleyyng worth a bene. (IV 1851–54)

Sometimes, though largely to be dismissed as a male fantasy, a young woman might lust after an old man who was not even rich. Gerald of Wales (late twelfth century) tells this tale: A young nun was consumed with desire for a saintly old monk named Gilbert. She confessed her desire to him. He cured her by giving a public sermon about resisting fornication in which he stripped and revealed his naked body, "hairy, thin, scabby and horrid. . . . The woman was by that remedy totally cured of her carnal desires."[12] Gilbert was, the story shows, immune to the flattery of being desired by the desirable. That Gilbert's thinness is right up there with scabbiness as elicitors of disgust probably indicates he was emaciated, but it also shows how what we often think of as objectively descriptive words like 'thin' that relate to body type are hard to translate accurately across the centuries to get at how flattering or unflattering they might be.

The sagas too, in their unique way, make comedy of the disgustingness of an old man sullying a young attractive woman. The disgust elicited by the *senex amans* (old lover) operates squarely in the comic register, the old man's inalienable human dignity pretty much tossed to the winds. The young woman's revulsion is, I suppose, to be supplied by inference. In the world of this saga, chronicling actual events in this case, a marriage of an old man and a young woman provokes a young man named Hall to abduct her. Even the saga writer joins the mirth by turning it into farce: "Hall said that an old man should not *pollute*[13] such a good-looking woman any longer, so he took her and the man's horse too. The horse was named Mani and was the best of all horses" (*Sturlu saga* 12:78). That is worthy of Chaucer in its ironies.

My last example is one wholly devoted to disgust, not to pathetic old lovers, but to the horror that awaits raw objectless sexual desire when the object of desire loses desirability once the urge has been satisfied. The account is so distasteful that I hesitate to present it, but, having said that, were I to withhold it, you would feel that I have toyed with you, and as you know, toying in the sense of amorous foreplay is often worthy of the disgustful description Hamlet gives it, when urging his mother not to do the act of darkness that night with Claudius:

> Not this, by no means, that I bid you do:
> Let the bloat king tempt you again to bed,
> Pinch wanton on your cheek, call you his mouse,
> And let him, for a pair of reechy kisses,
> Or paddling in your neck with his damn'd fingers. . . . (3.4.181–85)

Match that for uncompromising sex-loathing diction: bloat, pinch wanton, baby talk, stinking kisses, paddling in your neck (which means breasts) with damned fingers.

The tasteless example: Machiavelli is writing to his friend Luigi Guicciardini in 1509. He thinks his story will amuse his friend. Niccolò is forty at the time, hardly young himself, especially in the fifteenth and sixteenth centuries, though the old prostitute he describes may not be much older. Given the times, she is past any prime she may ever have had by some twenty years, to which we must add the ravages of the diseases that came with her work:

> I've been in [Verona] for three days, losing my discrimination because of conjugal famine, when I came upon an old woman who launders my shirts. . . . She asked me to be so kind as to enter her house for a moment, she wanted to show me some fine shirts. . . . So, naive prick that I am, I believed her and went in. . . . I made out in the gloom a woman cowering in the corner affecting modesty. . . . The old slut took me by the hand and led me over to her saying, "This is the shirt I wanted to sell you." . . . I, shy fellow that I am, was absolutely terrified; still to make a long story short, I fucked her. Although I found her thighs flabby . . . her breath stank a bit— nevertheless, hopelessly horny, I went to her with it. Once I had done it I [lit a lamp to take a look]. Ugh. I nearly dropped dead on the spot, that woman was so ugly. The first thing I noticed about her was a tuft of hair, part white, part black . . ., although the crown of her head was bald . . .; one eye looked up, the other down, and one was larger than the other; her tear ducts were full of mucus and she had no eyelashes. . . . One of her nostrils was sliced open and full of snot. . . . Her mouth . . . was twisted to one side, and from that side drool was oozing, because, since she was toothless, she could not hold back her saliva. Her upper lip sported a longish but skimpy moustache. . . . As I stood there absolutely . . . stupefied staring at this monster, she became aware of it and tried to say, "what's the matter, sir?" but she could not get it out because she stuttered. As soon as she opened her mouth, she exuded such a stench . . . that I threw up all over her. Having thus repaid her in kind I departed.[14]

Once his sexual urge had been sated, only pure revulsion remains. He blames his vomiting on breath that a few minutes earlier had not interfered with the sex act but seems now to be so aversive that it makes him puke. Here we have an image of what libido can overcome (though he may well be exaggerating what his succeeded in overcoming); it is hardly rare that part of the thrill of sex is what must be overcome to engage in it. Libido, more than love, is blind. It can render the disgustful alluring or ignorable. In its kind of feast-of-misrule way, disgust allows for a full mixing of jellies, as in the old blues idiom for fornication: jelly roll. There is here no happy folkloric ending as in the *Wife of Bath's Tale,* where the loathely old hag is transformed magically into a most fetching young lady.

Sorry, old men, no princess kissing you will change you from the frog you have become, and Machiavelli comes off worse than the old whore. One wonders about Machiavelli here, for whom one would think no word is not calculated, but he does not seem to recognize that he lost whatever moral battle was being waged by letting the whore have a voice, a faintly dignifying voice, a voice of concern, of fellow feeling. There is even something touching in that she might have some faint *amour propre*, where she does not see herself as disgusting as he does: "What's the matter, sir?" Supposedly, she only tried to get those words out but was unable to because she stuttered, but then he heard them nonetheless, and lets us hear her say them; he, it seems, says the words for her. It would be giving his unconscious too much credit were we to see him hearing her barely uttered words as an unconscious manifestation of guilt.[15] Nor does he seem to see that he gave her a modicum more dignity than he thinks he preserved for himself by playing the clown for his friend.

It is not good for an old person's self-esteem to become a living cautionary tale, but there is some solace, because the hyperfastidiousness that plagued me when young and that was in part overcome by having children and writing a book on disgust is now in old age overcome by the one kindness old age does you. The very means of engaging the disgusting, your *senses*, grow biblically dim and are no longer acute enough to pick up the odors and the sights or feel the slime that made you cringe and recoil when younger.

I can no longer smell bad smells and often have to be bullied by my wife to believe her that the dog needs a bath, that my shoes are bearing some dog's production, or that a skunk just sprayed in the backyard. All my senses are dulled. With smell goes taste. I am now omnivorous.

With age goes the ability to see things up close, to see the hairs coming out of places that horrify the young.

But if I have been a bit sour in this chapter, I want to conclude on a very positive note. The loss of cognitive abilities that accompanies the dulling of senses is like the first sip of a cup drawn from the River Lethe. Now when you make a fool of yourself, shame yourself, give a bad talk, or disappoint the audience, days later you have a hard time remembering that it occurred. Forgetfulness swallows self-loathing.

We confirm in our old age the ancient trope of senescence as a second childhood, and where more than in our inability to be sensitive to the disgusting? Just as you were immune to disgust when you were six months old, before you could entertain ideas of contamination, contagion, and impurity, so are you fast becoming immune to it now. When at last we sink from mere old age into dementia and senility, we do not even care that we are now likely to be back in nappies, or what I as an American call diapers, and we can no longer speak either, having suffered a stroke. We play our last scene as Jacques describes it in *As You Like It*, so often quoted: "sans teeth, sans eyes, sans taste, sans everything."

5

The Messenger

THIS CHAPTER, LIKE THE last, deals with a kind of fluidity, but in an examination not of bodily substances and bodies themselves but of one particular social role a body might play. It began as a talk given at the University of Münster in December 2008, as part of a series of lectures on mediation organized by the medievalist Professor Gerd Althoff in connection with the city of Münster honoring Kofi Annan with the Westphalian Peace Award. As you might now expect, I took a less-than-celebratory view of mediation and looked at aspects of its grayer side. I found an email I sent to my wife upon arrival in Münster, which reveals a partial reenactment of the incident at All Souls told in the introduction:

> plane got in early, so i caught an earlier train but had to stand for two hours, no seats. i spilled red wine all over my jeans which are now next to worthless. i just took a shower with them on. i will rest an hour and then call gerd althoff . . .

Now to serious matters.

The difference between negotiation and mediation by conventional formal criteria is whether there are two parties or three. But sometimes it is hard to count to three with confidence.[1] It is not always clear just how 'third' a third party is, even though many wish to paint an ideal portrait of the mediator as impartial, or equally obliged to both sides, or serving a community interest judged to be in moral and practical terms more enlightened, less twisted by self-interest and passion than if the matter were left to the unaided principal parties to hammer out their differences by negotiation or violence, violent encounters being, also, a negotiation of sorts.[2] A mediator's force is claimed to be mostly a moral force, aided by his rhetorical skills or by his personal ability to cajole, flatter, or threaten, for by definition he is without formal authority to impose a settlement. He is not a judge or an arbitrator.

The thirdness of an arbitrator or judge is less ambiguous than the thirdness of mediators, precisely because arbitrators and judges have a clearly defined power to issue a decision. The mediator's force is much fuzzier. 'Thirdness' is so fundamental to the essence of the judge or arbitrator that it informs the philology of the words for *judge* or *arbitrator* in more than a few languages: thus in Old Norse an arbitrator is sometimes called an *oddman* (*oddamaðr*), *odd*[3] being the word for the point of a triangle and from which English takes its word for uneven numbers. The English word *umpire* makes the same move: it was borrowed from French in the thirteenth century where it was *noumpere*,[4] that is, *non peer*, not equal, the odd man, the third party. And in modern Hebrew the verb to arbitrate is formed from the root for three: 'to three' is to arbitrate.[5] There is no such clarity of thirdness in mediation.

The terms *mediators/mediation*, as I have already indicated, tend to carry with them a positive moral valence. Mediation has come to suggest the values of peace, or in the idiom of self-esteem therapy, it is about the 'empowerment' of claimants who are otherwise excluded from more expensive forms of dispute resolution that require lawyers and courts. And should a mediator be worthy of being called an intercessor,[6] his moral stock rises even higher. 'Intercessor' evokes images of Christ, Mary, or the saints mediating between a frightened and sinful humanity and a Dangerous Divinity. Mediation is talked about with much piety and celebration; mediators are esteemed as the peacemakers blessed in the Beatitudes.[7]

But mediation has a darker side. An intercessor, a mediator, for instance, is a go-between, which in English has a suspect, even immoral sense. Or he is more neutrally a broker, bringing a buyer and a seller together, a middle man. But the go-between in English is also a pimp, a procurer of prostitutes. The ever-perspicacious Canadian social theorist Erving Goffman treats mediators as playing what he calls a 'discrepant role':

> The go-between or mediator . . . learns the secrets of each side and gives each side the true impression that he will keep its secrets; but he tends to give each side the false impression that he is more loyal to it than to the other. . . . As an individual, the go-between's activity is bizarre, untenable, and undignified, vacillating as it does from one set of appearances and loyalties to another. The go-between can be thought of simply as a double-shill.[8]

Mediators, in short, need not be all that honest, in fact, probably cannot be all that honest and be successful; they might in some of their avatars be talebearers and spies. The historical record is so dense with examples of the dark side of mediation that one need not look long to find examples. It is hardly shocking to anyone to discover that mediators had their own interests to advance; they often benefited not just by gaining honor as a peacemaker but also by arranging a settlement that weakened the disputants, who were often also the mediator's competitors.

What I aim to do in this chapter is to examine the embryology of mediation, the moment at which one party starts to split in two, as in the earliest cell divisions of an organism, and then when two parties start to metamorphose into three, without it necessarily ever becoming analytically clear if a particular person is truly a principal or an agent, or a third party. I want to focus on the messenger, for it is in the simple messenger that we find the origins of the grandest of mediators, the saints and Christ. The messenger is the Ur-mediator.

Take a messenger sent by A to B whom B then sends back to A with an answer. The messenger starts out as an agent of A; he may be a high-ranking official in his household, or he may be a lowly servant. Surely the status of the person asked to carry the message will depend on variables such as the absolute status of B, the relative status of A and B, the content of the message, whether good or bad news, and its purpose—whether a request for a favor, an order, a claim, an offer of marriage, or a demand for or an offer of capitulation. But when the messenger bears B's answer back to A, he is then acting, at least in part, as B's agent. He is thus a double agent.

'Double agent' here has a double sense: in its benign sense, it merely describes a person who is the agent of two principals, in this case of A and B. But such a double agent is now also in the suspect structural position of serving two masters whose interests may be in conflict. He may now be tempted to be a double agent in the nefarious sense of being a specialist in betrayal. There are thus more than a few reasons why one might want to kill the messenger beyond making him the scapegoat for the bad news he delivers. It might well be that the messenger himself is the bad news. Duplicity is built into the structure of being a go-between. It is no wonder that Hermes, the messenger of the gods, is a trickster and the patron of thieves and conmen, or that Virgil says of Iris, Juno's messenger, that she was "well acquainted with causing harm" (*Aeneid* 5.618).

These issues reside at the very core of the mystery of the Incarnation. Could there be a better example of the conflation of principal and agent than in Jesus, the preeminent go-between? He is a double agent, as God and as man, whose very distinguishability from the Principal who sent him and from mankind who sent him back was a matter of endless debate, of heresies and schisms: was he one or two, more man than God, more God than man? (And what of that message-bearing dove to add more difficulty to the mix?) The Incarnation manifests all the ambiguities that haunt mediation and the go-between. Exactly whom is he working for? And what's in it for him?

Our simple messenger, who began as an agent of the sender, is now in the position of becoming more fully realized as an agent in his own right in the philosophical sense of being a decision-making actor. He has choices of his own to make, temptations to resist, risks to bear, and he can find that there is a world of possibility in the routine task of bearing messages or objects back and forth.

Even a mere courier, a postman, can become an agent in the philosophical sense. Couriers bearing messages between Swiss towns in the fifteenth and sixteenth centuries were given gifts by the recipients; these gifts were a big part of the courier's income.[9] Evidence shows that the value of the gift was often proportionate to the weightiness of the message, even when the news was bad. Surely this gave messengers some inducement to exaggerate both triumphs and losses. A simple courier might start to play with the content of his message, and if his message was a written dispatch, that by itself need not prevent him from providing an oral gloss. People were well aware of such possibilities. Samuel Pepys tells of a Dutch renegade who bears a false tale of Dutch atrocities committed against the English in hopes, it is alleged, of some reward from the English. Observes Pepys: "the world doth think that there is some design on one side or other, either of the Dutch or French—for it is not likely a fellow would invent such a lie to get money, whereas he might have hoped for a better reward by telling something in behalf of us to please us" (Feb. 25, 1665).[10]

There are also freelancing messengers, who are not agents of anyone in particular. In saga Iceland we find beggarwomen and other vagabonds bearing tales from farm to farm, knowing that they will be rewarded for bearing malicious gossip, not always false. They even try to prompt the slanderous statements that they truthfully bear to the insulted person.[11] Freelancing go-betweens need not be peacemakers, so beloved of the dispute-processing literature; they can also be talebearers and fomenters of strife, cursed by moralists from the beginning of time. But talebearers too are mediators after a fashion, and surely mediators are talebearers.

Though the messenger is not quite the classic mediator, still it is undeniable that even the highest-status mediator is a messenger of sorts. A bearer of words, back and forth. If he has a bit of the devil in him, he can also be something of an angel: our word *angel* obscures the fact that angel is merely the translation of the Hebrew word for messenger (*mal'akh*) into Greek and subsequently Latinized and Germanicized. *Mal'akh* applied equally if he were sent by God, or by King Saul, or by any old farmer.[12]

The root of *mal'akh*—*l'kh*—also figures in the word for task or work: *mla'kha*. The root sense of *l'kh* is something like 'to send (bearing a message)' but comes to be generalized to mean any task.[13] Now consider the Akkadian word (the Semitic language of ancient Babylon and Assyria) for message, letter, messenger: *shipru*. It too derives from a root meaning to send a message, *spr*, and also comes to generate a related form meaning task or work, thus showing the same semantic generative properties of Hebrew *l'kh*.[14] In Hebrew the *spr* root generates the word for book, letter, or document and the verb for to tell, narrate, or count, all obviously relevant to message bearing. I hardly wish to make too much of this but, as we see, there is in the Semitic languages a semantic constellation that finds in message bearing the very archetype of a task. Add a dose of Neoplatonic Christianizing and then it is less of a wonder that in the beginning was the Word, and the Word does the Work, the Task, of creation in the Gospel of John.

Even in the Indo-European languages there is a link between message bearing and the notion of task, job, or the undertaking of specific enterprises. Take the Carolingian *missi*, the messengers of the king, who go on *missi*ons. The word *mission* comes to mean the business that the *missus*, or messenger, is to carry out. He is on a mission, we say, and eventually in the jargon of the US military, mission comes to mean a particular operation, the task at hand. Mission Impossible. Thus too it is a *missionary* who bears the word, the message of God, so that he becomes an *imitatio Christi,* imitating Jesus as message bearer who himself is the message as well as the mediator between God and sinful humanity.

In the Hebrew Bible, or in the remarkable Amarna letters from 1300 BCE Egypt, or in the chronicles and letters of the preindustrial ages, one could not avoid noticing that no one takes messengers for granted. They are frequently mentioned, and often named. One of the dominant themes of the Amarna letters is the messengers themselves. Why have you detained them? Why do you not admit them? Why have you sent none to me? Why do your messengers lie to you? The Babylonian king says this to Pharaoh:

> Previously my father would send a messenger to you and you would not detain him for long. You quickly sent him off, and you would also send here to my father a beautiful greeting gift. But now when I sent a messenger to you, you have detained him for six years and you have sent me as my greeting gift, the only thing in six years, 30 minas of gold that look like silver. (EA 3)[15]

A letter from Tushratta, the king of Mittani,[16] to Pharaoh indicates that Mane, Pharaoh's messenger, is being well treated; he "is not dying.

Truly, he is just the same" (EA 20).[17] Tushratta comes to value Mane greatly and so writes sometime later after Mane has returned to Egypt:

> Mane your envoy is very good; there does not exist a man like him in all the world. . . . And may my brother not detain my envoys. . . . And my envoys may my brother let go as fast as possible. . . . My brother may say: "You yourself have also detained my envoys." No, I have not detained them. . . . May my brother let my envoys go as soon as possible so they can leave. And may my brother send Mane along, so he can leave together with my envoy. Any other envoy may my brother not send. May he send only Mane. If my brother does not send Mane and sends someone else I do not want him and my brother should know it. No. May my brother send Mane. (EA24)

The messenger, Mane, the go-between, has become himself the subject of the negotiation; he, as well as the amount of the marriage portion in this case, is the scarce item over which the parties are bargaining. Such has become Mane's standing with the king to whom he has been sent that it would be no longer accurate to describe him merely as an agent of the first party, Pharaoh, whose officer he is. The king of Mittani has come to think of him as one of his own, precisely because he knows he is also dear to Pharaoh. By being so esteemed, by being a very successful double agent, Mane has become something like a third party.

Mane is clearly a man of high rank, a messenger fit to travel back and forth between rulers. And because he is of high rank and has a certain credibility, he is also, as were all the messengers whose detainment is lamented by Tushratta, not just a courier or ambassador, but a hostage.

It is often noted from ancient Sumer to sixteenth-century Florence and beyond that messengers are treated to sumptuous hospitality. Let Tushratta vouch again: "Mane my brother's messenger and Hane, my brother's interpreter, I have exalted like gods. I have given them many gifts and treated them very kindly for their report was excellent" (EA, 21). Recall what I said about the incentives a messenger has to elaborate in the message so as to please the recipient. Tushratta is quite frank about the quality of Mane's hospitality being correlated to the quality of the message he bore. Messengers are also guests, sometimes captive guests to be sure, but the norms of hospitality mean they are to be feted, and sometimes feted and feted, before they are even allowed to state their business. (Treat yourself to the remarkable letter, more than 4,000 years old, reproduced in the footnote that ends this sentence.[18])

In the Icelandic sagas, for instance, it is rare for a person arriving bearing news, or on business, to state the reasons for his coming until the next day. The protocol suggests that it is improper for the host even to ask why he has come. Sometimes a host, bewildered when his guest does not state a reason for his visit the next morning, must finally assert himself and ask to what he owes the visit.[19] One of the benefits of showing sumptuous hospitality was that it put the guest in an awkward position, for now he was in the host's debt, and thus in situations where the messenger was also something of an envoy with terms to negotiate, his bargaining strength was compromised.[20]

Fulfilling the proper forms of good hosting must have been hard given a desire to know what the substance of the missive was. What if the matter were urgent? Urgency has to mean something different when the time it takes to deliver news is measured in months, not in microseconds. If a message took two months to get from the Nile to Nineveh, one could wait a day or two to talk business; it would mean waiting no more than to pause for a breath before stating one's business nowadays. True, fire signals on mountaintops could get messages delivered much faster, but the informational content of such signals was rather limited—either the enemy is coming, get ready, quick, or we won, hurray. Moreover, the enemy, as Thucydides notes (3.22), could make the signals meaningless by lighting competing fires, reducing what might have been a meaningful message to mere noise; whose fire was whose?

The feting of messengers could go terribly wrong too, not because of competitiveness over seating arrangements, as we have seen, but because the rules of proper behavior got lost in translation. Herodotus tells of Persian envoys visiting Macedonia who complain that the feast welcoming them had no women present. To entertain us properly there should be women, they say; among us, there are women present. The Macedonians answer that it is not their custom to feast in mixed company but reluctantly oblige the guests, who then complain that the women are not sitting next to them, which request is also obliged. After the Persian envoys start fondling the women's breasts, the Persians are killed in a bed-trick where the Macedonian hosts substitute armed adolescent boys for the girls (5.18–21).

Sometimes a messenger was not feted but deliberately insulted, thrown into prison, beaten or killed, or kept under house arrest, as we saw when the king of Babylon complained of detaining his messenger for six years.[21] When Wenamun, an Egyptian on a mission to Byblos about 1075 BCE, begs to leave, the king of Byblos answers thus: "'Indeed, I have not done to you what was done to the envoys of Khaemwese, after they had spent seventeen years (!) in this land . . .' And he said to his butler: 'take him to see the tomb where they lie.'"[22] When David sends emissaries to Hanun, king of the Ammonites, to console Hanun on the death of Hanun's father, Hanun has half the beards of David's men shaved off, and their clothing cut to expose their buttocks. The messengers were mortified, and David in solicitude tells them to lay low in Jericho until their beards grow back (2 Sam. 10.1–5). When in Merovingian times (here sixth century CE) high-ranking legates from King Chilperic—Bishop Egidius and Duke Guntram Boso—have a contentious bargaining session with King Guntram, they are shown the door with excrement and filth dumped on them.[23] A Hittite treaty from c. 1400 BCE finds it necessary to include a provision against plying messengers with truth serum: "He must not ensnare [the messengers] by means of a magical plant."[24]

Being a messenger was not the most enviable of tasks, unless you had the fortune to bear good tidings. Even then there were the dangers of the road—bandits, disease, bad weather, toll takers, palace bureaucrats serving as official and unofficial gatekeepers—so that when you got there you might not be able to deliver your message without paying substantial bribes. But should you not be bearing good tidings, your arrival could often occasion bigger risks than the usual ones of the road. The plot of the *Chanson de Roland*, no less than the plot of the Incarnation, depends on the assumption that volunteering someone to be a messenger between hostile parties was like offering the person up for slaughter. Message delivery was often heroic duty or a fool's errand. Thus the opening stanza of Robert Frost's poem that bears the title of its first line:

> The bearer of evil tidings,
> When he was halfway there,
> Remembered that evil tidings
> Were a dangerous thing to bear.

Frost's messenger decides to head elsewhere.

There was an understanding that varied from culture to culture of diplomatic immunity when messengers were passing between openly hostile parties. It seems the immunity was fairly weak among the ancient Semites, less so among the Greeks or Franks, with their staffs and wands to mark them as entitled to safe conduct.[25] But neither the Spartans nor the Athenians dealt kindly with the envoys Darius sent to them to demand that they submit to him. The ones sent to Athens were thrown into a pit, the ones to Sparta pushed into a well.[26] The Spartans tried to make amends years later to Xerxes, Darius's son, for their breach of heraldic immunity. They sent him, in atonement, two men of good family for Xerxes to put to death. Xerxes, an astute psychologist, sent them back alive, noting nicely that he was not going to behave as badly to emissaries as the Spartans did, nor was he about to free them of their burden of guilt for their crime.[27]

There were messengers no one wanted to see; these are the ones who came as tax collectors, tribute takers, or summoners, who often thought it prudent to arrive well accompanied and heavily armed. More than a few messengers of higher status in the medieval chronicles designated as envoys, legates, and government officials (*nuntii, legati, missi*) bring small armies to deliver their messages.[28] Bearing bad news to a hostile party is obviously dangerous business, but the paradigm case of killing the messenger is when the messenger bears bad news back to his *own* people. One wonders what possibly could induce the man so charged to carry out his mission. Or who would be so unwise as to return home as a sole survivor? When the only Athenian to survive a battle against the Aegintans returns and tells of the debacle, "the wives of the men who had gone on the expedition to Aegina . . . were so appalled that he alone of the entire expedition had been spared that they surrounded the man, grabbed hold of him and stabbed him with the brooches they used to fasten their robes, each of them in turn asking him as they did so where their husband was. So he was dispatched" (Herodotus, 5.87–89).

Lords sent messengers to bear good news whom they meant to reward, and messengers to bear bad news who were expendable. When Joab sends a messenger to David whom Joab knows he is putting at risk because the news is mixed, he makes sure to give the messenger a saving clause at the end of the message that will spare him: Joab charged the messenger, saying, "When thou hast made an end of telling the matters of the war unto the king, And if so be that the king's wrath arise, and he say unto thee, 'Wherefore approached ye so nigh unto the city when ye did fight? knew ye not that they would shoot from the wall? . . . why went ye nigh the wall?' then say thou, 'Thy servant Uriah the Hittite is dead also' " (2 Sam. 11.19–21).[29]

There is an indication in the sagas that people dressed in certain ways or took certain paths depending on the quality of their message. Although it is hard to get at this in the sources, there may have been a color coding of clothing to prepare the recipients for bad news so that it would not lead to an overhasty emotional response lethal to the messenger. In more than a few cases in the Bible, messengers bearing bad tidings adopted ritualized humiliation markers: torn clothing, dirt or ashes heaped on their heads (e.g., 1 Sam. 4.12; 2 Sam. 1.2). I suspect they hoped that this might save them.[30]

A prophet is a messenger of sorts too. He often bore doom-laden evil tidings that were quite dangerous to bear. Prophets, like any other messenger, might be tempted to alter their messages in ways pleasing to their addressees. It took guts to deliver bad news. Jonah runs away; Jeremiah tries to beg off from what he understands is a dangerous calling (Jer. 1.7–8, 17–19). The dangers of bearing bad news are the core of Jeremiah's test for determining a true prophet from a false one. A true prophet bears messages you do not want to hear; tells you of doom, not of peace; and does not play to your desires to think positively and to look on the bright side (28.8–9). If he is a true prophet he must possess an almost willful desire to act against what others would readily understand as his self-interest. This might help explain Jesus's willfully walking into the shadow of the valley of his own death, perhaps to compensate for offering too much 'good news,' which in Jeremiah's terms indicates a false prophet. Jeremiah gets beaten up and thrown into prison (37.15–16).

In some cases, though, it might be good policy to kill messengers bearing news of a defeat or of a battle going badly. Raimondo

Montecuccoli, an Imperial general, and the hero of the battle of Szentgotthárd in 1664, who wrote perceptively about war and generalship, notes instances of battle leaders killing the messenger bearing bad tidings, not because of a belief that the messenger bore some causal responsibility for the events he reported, but because the messenger was acting with culpable carelessness, given the knowledge he should have about how fragile an army's courage is and that any news that might undo its courage must be suppressed.[31]

The point Raimondo makes is that it is incumbent on the messenger bearing ill tidings to make sure he gives out one message for public consumption and whispers his honest assessment into the ear of the leader in private. That is the reason Yahweh kills the spies who return from Canaan announcing the invincibility of its occupants: "And there we saw the giants (Nephilim), the sons of Anak, which come of the giants: and we were in our own sight as grasshoppers, and so we were in their sight" (Num. 13.33). The message demoralizes the Israelites who now lament, yet again, that they ever left Egypt. The spies' culpability was more than just their cowardice, which revealed their insufficient faith in Yahweh's might, but rather that their message demoralized the entire nation.

It is precisely to demoralize the recipients that a hostile messenger bearing bad tidings to the enemy might well wish to have his message overheard: thus the desperate attempt of King Hezekiah's main minister to have Sennacharib's messengers not speak in Hebrew ("the Jews' language") but in Aramaic, so the commoners on the walls would not understand the dire message (2 Kings 18.26–27).[32] The chief Assyrian messenger the Rab'shakeh will have none of it; he answers brutally, and obviously in Hebrew, threatening a siege: "Hath my master sent me to thy master, and to thee, to speak these words? hath he not sent me to the men which sit on the wall, that they may eat their own dung, and drink their own piss with you." Nasty wit, we see, is a virtue in certain high-status messengers; it got the Rab'shakeh immortalized in his enemy's historical record no less, not once but twice, for the same scene also appears in Isaiah (Is. 36).[33]

Aristotle gives us another reason for rightly blaming the messenger: his not caring not to cause pain.[34] Yet we have an inscription on a tomb from 1500 BCE Egypt of someone who took pride in not killing messengers bearing bad news: "I did not confuse the report with the reporter. . . . I was a model of kindliness."[35] Apparently the baseline expectation was to kill the messenger.

Woe to the messenger who is the subject of the message he bears, unless he knows, like Mane, that the contents are flattering to him: Uriah the Hittite, Rosencrantz and Guildenstern, these messengers are very much in the dark, and have to be, for they are bearing their own death warrants. A Sumerian myth (3rd millennium BCE) attributes the invention of the envelope to this kind of letter.[36]

A messenger had to know how to deliver good news too, for if too good, it might sound "too good to be true." Herodotus tells of a messenger from Samos who reports to the Greek commanders how vulnerable the Persians are to an immediate attack. To convince the Greeks that he is telling the truth, he offers himself either as a hostage or to join the fight (9.90–91). This raises some interesting problems for a mediator, and for a messenger: how to make yourself believable is no different for the liar than it is for the truth teller.[37]

You could also get killed for delivering good news, if you were mistaken about how it would be received. The messenger who thought David wanted to hear that Saul was dead is one (2 Sam. 4.10); Jesus, perhaps, in some respects, is another, for only a subset of his addressees liked the message.

The dangers were not all the messenger's. The recipients of messages also bore risks even when they were more powerful than the sender. Take the case of Ehud in Judges 3.15–30. Israel had been a tributary of Moab for eighteen years. It was Ehud's duty to bear the Israelite tribute to Eglon, king of Moab. After handing over the tribute, Ehud tells Eglon he has a secret message to deliver. Eglon dismisses his attendants; Ehud draws near: "I have a message from God for you" (RSV), he says, as he draws a hidden short sword and plunges it into Eglon's guts, whose folds of fat completely engulf the sword. Ehud departs, closing the door behind him. Eglon's servants assume Eglon is relieving himself and so do not check up on him until Ehud has gotten away.

If it is the rare messenger who is an assassin, it is the not-so-rare assassin who poses, indeed might *be*, as Ehud shows, a messenger. The messenger is the assassin of choice for Queen Fredegund in Gregory of Tour's history.[38] Saul too sends messengers, *ml'achim*, to kill David (1

Sam. 19.11), angels of death so to speak. Being a messenger was replete with dangers, but so, we see, was getting a message. English still pays homage to this with the cold sneer: "Did ya get the message?" Eglon sure did. Israel was not going to be sending more tribute; relations with Moab had been redefined.

Contrast the case in which the recipient is much weaker than the sender and is by virtue of his weakness inclined to read even a benign request from the messenger as a threat. When Naaman, stricken with leprosy, bears a letter from his king, the king of Aram, to the king of Israel (most likely Jehoram, son of Ahab), asking him in all innocence to see to a cure for Naaman, given that he has heard that there is a prophet in Israel (Elisha) who can effect a cure, the king of Israel rends his clothes in despair. He assumes the request is a setup, an excuse for Aram to invade, to exact more tribute, by asking for the impossible (2 Kings 5.7). The story provides a nice indication that not everyone was inclined to believe in routine miracles performed by famed miracle workers such as Elisha. (This story happened to be my Bar Mitzvah portion, which I chanted nervously before our small congregation in Green Bay in spring 1959, as I was transformed by so doing from a boy to a juridical man.)

Ehud's one-liner—"I have a message from God for you"—would suit a Mafia movie. The lethality of Ehud's message could hardly be clearer. The letter killeth, as Paul says (2 Cor. 3.6), in more ways than one. Ehud's wit is not just the stuff of good stories. He plays the prophet bearing messages from God, and he plays off Eglon's expectation that he is about to play double agent in Eglon's favor by giving him some important secret information. The levels of dark expectation and ambiguity make this a delicious scene, for the understanding is that messengers will have more information than that which they are officially charged to deliver. It is not surprising, in other words, that a messenger might betray his sender, might even be expected to.

The prospect of his messenger double-dealing might well be part of the price the sender has to pay to get good information on the messenger's return, for messengers are nothing if not spies. Even innocent messengers have eyes and ears and will be questioned as to what they saw back home by the recipient, and by their masters when they return. Thus, it might be a wise strategy to stage false fronts for the messenger before he departed, deliberately misinforming him before sending him off.

A messenger could not help but be a spy even if he did not want to be, even if he had no evil intentions. No wonder those ancient Near Eastern kings 'entertained' the messengers they received for three, six, seventeen years. A messenger had to make sure that his host believed the purpose of his mission was in fact its official purpose lest he be treated as a spy rather than as a messenger. Recall David's emissaries sent home half naked and half shaved. The reason they were so ill-treated is that it was claimed by Hanun's men that their visit was a pretense, and that spying was their true purpose. Suetonius reports of Augustus that at the beginning of his reign he kept in touch with provincial affairs by relays of runners spaced along the highway, but that he later organized a chariot service, "which proved the more satisfactory arrangement *because post-boys can be cross-examined on the situation* as well as delivering written messages."[39] One of the many advantages of employing pigeons to deliver messages was not only their speed but also that they couldn't be bribed into betraying the sender's interests, for the birds' interests (getting home) were exactly what was mobilized on behalf of the sender. Only humans, not pigeons, could be stool pigeons.

A passage from a tract of Egyptian wisdom literature (c. 1800 BCE) is directed to messengers:

> If you are a man of close trust,
> Whom one great man sends to another great man,
> Be entirely exact when he sends you.
> Do the commission for him as he says.
> Beware of making evil with a speech
> Which embroils one great man with another great man;
> Hold fast to Truth! Do not exceed it!
> An outburst is not to be repeated;
> Do not speak out against anyone,
> Great or small, it is a horror to the spirit.[40]

The messenger is told to stick to his text, exactly, but he is also to exercise discretion, especially about suppressing certain matters. If your master, the sender, was angry and said some ill-advised things, you should keep quiet about it. You are not to overstate, and you are to slant your account in favor of peacefulness and good relations. Here too the suggestion is that the messenger will be milked for information and will be asked to talk outside his text. Even the simplest messenger is thus on the way to becoming an ambassador, a negotiator, and, as this text supposes, a mediator between one great man and another, at the risk of his also being a traitor. To limit a freewheeling messenger, the following provision is added to a Hittite treaty, c. 1400 BCE: "If the words of the messenger are in agreement with the words of the tablet, trust the messenger. . . . But if the words of the speech of the messenger are not in agreement with the words of the tablet, you . . . shall certainly not trust the messenger, and shall certainly not take to heart the evil content of his report."[41]

The fact that the messenger will be thought to possess more knowledge than that which he has been officially charged to convey leads Montaigne, who did some messaging service in the civil wars of religion, to observe that he wants to be nothing more than a carrier pigeon; he wants no knowledge outside the text he is to deliver; he prefers to be in the dark:

> I know that everyone rebels if the deeper implications of the negotiations he is employed on are concealed from him and if some ulterior motive is secreted away. Personally I am glad if princes tell me no more than they want me to get on with; I have no desire that what I know should impede or constrain what I have to say. If I have to serve as a means of deception let at least my own conscience be safeguarded.[42]

Since the messenger will be queried beyond his text, he has the power to betray his sender advertently by revealing more than he should, or inadvertently, by being cajoled with drink, women or boys, and flattery. He also may be tortured into revealing what he knows if the softer persuasions do not work. That is why Themistocles, who himself knew a thing or two about betrayal (he was always cutting private deals with the enemy), sends men as messengers whom, Herodotus says, "he could rely upon, even were they to be put to the very extremes of torture, not to reveal the message which he had ordered them to communicate to the King" (8.110). No wonder Augustus got rid of his post boys.

There are other ways the sender is partly at the mercy of his messenger's interests. Classic tales are devoted to the theme. Gregory of Tours tells of a certain man who, in hopes of having his countship renewed, sent his son with gifts to King Guntram to plead on his behalf. But the son, by means of his father's gifts, got the office for himself, supplanting his father whose cause, Gregory says, he should have been supporting (4.42). The classic instance is the proxy wooer getting the girl for himself instead of for his principal. Rostand's Cyrano de Bergerac has no self-serving motives at all, but La Rochefoucauld notes another risk—that the messenger's very desire to gain glory in the successful accomplishment of his mission will lead him to lose sight of the principal's interest: "The reason why we frequently criticize those who act on our behalf is that almost always they lose sight of their friends' interest in the interest of the negotiation itself, which they make their own concern for the honor and glory of having succeeded in what they have undertaken" (Maxim 278).

There is an array of possibilities that governs the relationship between the sender and the messenger. Some messengers are clearly official and even bear powers to bind the principal, as when they are styled legates; some are official but merely message carriers without any other powers; some are unofficial, or operate on their own motion, to be claimed as messengers by the unofficial sender if the mission is successful, to be denied if it is not. There are a multitude of points that can be occupied on an 'officialness' scale.[43]

An ingenious Icelandic tale shows how a very cagey king might send a messenger without ever officially acknowledging that the person sent was a messenger, let alone *his* messenger. In this case Harald Hardradi of Norway simply lets an Icelander who wishes to give a polar bear to King Svein of Denmark carry on with his mission, even though Harald is tempted to confiscate the bear and kill the Icelander, for Harald and Svein are at war. By merely letting the Icelander continue on his way Harald sends a message, a peace feeler, that has the great virtue of being deniable as having been made should it fail to work. The Danish king is equally adept at sending the Icelander back to Harald but maintaining all deniability that the Icelander is now acting as *his* messenger.[44]

If this Icelander was a deniable messenger, we also have a class of messengers we think of as secret messengers, who also must operate outside certain official channels of message delivery and receipt, and who, in addition to the standard risks borne by a regular messenger, must bear the added ones of discovery.

In the standard sending of a message, the sender is of higher rank than the messenger. Message bearing is a service that is burdensome and dangerous. It might be better to send someone to do the job whom you can boss around. God's angels provide the best example: they are nothing but messengers (remember that that is the meaning of the word *angel*). In the Hebrew Bible they don't even have names—with two exceptions: Gabriel and Michael in the late Book of Daniel. Angels are manifestly God's inferiors. The messenger's structural inferiority to the sender provides the ammunition for an argument against Jesus's divinity made to Gregory of Tours by a certain Arian, Agilan, who himself was a messenger, a *legatus*, from the Visigothic king to King Chilperic: "No one sends a person who is not his own inferior," Agilan says, greatly angering Gregory. "God is he who sends; he who is sent is not God" (5.43). Gregory has arguments to oppose this, but he does not deny the force of Agilan's example, only countering that the Father also did the bidding of the Son, as when he raised Lazarus. But then so might any mere mortal be said to have had God do his bidding if his prayers were answered.[45]

But is Agilan right? There are special cases where the sender may be lower in rank than the message bearer, and this brings us back at long last to mediation, or more particularly to intercession. A lowly petitioner, to get his message to the person he desires to have access to, might not just have to use one intermediary, but a whole series of them. He seeks out first his own higher-status kinsman, who then seeks out his lord, who is a cousin of the bishop, and the bishop gains access to the archbishop, who goes to the king.[46] Each person asks a favor of one higher up the food chain and each serves as a messenger who is higher in status than his immediate sender. Intercessors, we might say, are a subclass of mediators, and also a subclass of message bearers, who trade on whom they know and the gates they can enter. Though in one sense they are the agents of the lowly principals who are the petitioners, in fact, the petitioners usually have to pay or pray to get the intercessor to intercede, and often pay *and* pray, as when one invokes the saints or the gods.[47]

One further wrinkle. With email and texting we are often our own messengers and many of the same risks arise. More than a few of you have, I bet, pressed reply to a message not intended for the message sender but that you meant to forward to a third party with a comment that you would have greatly preferred the original message sender never to see. You as messenger have hung yourself as message sender out to dry. When I attached "just what you would expect from a cowardly jerk like X" to X's missive to me, but pressed reply instead of forwarding it as I had intended to my friend Y—oh well, one friendship terminated. If I had wanted to shoot the messenger for screwing up like that, I would have had to commit suicide.

In the book I wrote on disgust I talked about a class of people I called "moral menials." These are people whose socially necessary jobs are somewhat distasteful, often demanding morally suspect action and accommodating consciences that do not stand in their way—lawyers, politicians, and hangmen are obvious examples. But there are more: we might have to add the mediator, the message bearer, the intervener, all perhaps morally suspect by having to go between, by being placed in the middle of things.

There is another point I wish to recall, which I started this chapter with. It was the ambiguity of the thirdness of the so-called third party, who often starts as an agent of one of the principals, and then must also work for the other party to carry out his task for the first party who employed him. Even the simplest courier puts himself and us, as I said more than once, in the world of double agents. True thirdness, complete independence from either party, is rare, a prerogative of a mighty intervener who can force himself between the parties whether they like it or not. But watch how in saga Iceland this intervener's ability to make peace is accomplished by relinquishing his thirdness. In several saga cases we find a third-party peacemaker who insists that the contenders put down their weapons and stop fighting, saying: "I will join the first party that listens to me."[48] In other words, the mediating peacemaker can only be effective as a third party, by threatening to abandon that role and becoming a first or second party.

It is standard knowledge among anthropologists and medieval historians that peacemakers are often drawn from the ranks of the contending parties, who have changed their minds about the relation of risks to rewards of continuing the quarrel. So when we move from two parties to three, from negotiation to mediation, let us recognize that the third party is, as the Old Norse would have it, an 'odd man,' caught in a regress of ambiguity and shifting alignments, and who can be located on a point anywhere from principal to agent, from first to second to third party. He subsumes, if not as sacredly, the mysteries of three persons in one of the Trinity.

6

A Jaundiced View of Authenticity (and Identity)

THE EMBRYOLOGY OF THIS chapter requires an explanation. It is a substantial revision of a keynote address I gave at a conference on authenticity in May 2017 at the University of Freiburg (im Breisgau). I am not especially well informed in the relevant philosophical and social science literature on authenticity, but evidently the invitation was owing to my having written a book called *Faking It,* which dealt with the self-doubts that make us, or me, often feel like a fraud, or, less grandly, as not quite convincingly managing the proper social and psychological motions demanded by the moment. My 'authenticity' has more its folk sense, one that normal people think of when they reference Polonius's "this above all to thine own self be true."

A good half of the talk was cribbed from *Faking It* and for that reason I would not have included it in this book had not that very cribbing provoked the gods to humiliate me as they had at All Souls (pp. 4–6). A conference participant caught me dead out in an error that exposed me as a pretentiously incompetent fool. The ironies of this occurring at a conference on authenticity are apparent, and of course I had to revise substantially much of what I had recycled in self-satisfied laziness from *Faking It.* As an act of penance, I give you this authentic wee *cri du coeur.*

I.

One problem with authenticity as a topic is narrowing the domain of the relevant. It is close to issues of truth and falsity though not completely congruent with them; it is intimately tied to matters of sincerity, motive, character, hypocrisy, and competence, but not wholly subsumed by them. It may or may not be tied to issues of proof, knowledge, and verifiability; and the word or concept seems equally applicable to objects, character, deeds, performances of music, and emotions and other inner states. In one problematic domain it seems to invite attention to the 'self,' that philosophical and psychological mystery: what it is, or even if it is, and if it is, whether it is accessible, or whether better accessible by others or by oneself, all so as to determine the nearly indeterminable issue of whether one is true to it or not. If we accept that we have an actual self, is it clear that we have only one? These do not admit of easy answers, if they admit of any.

Add that we are social beings and are forced to play a variety of roles and thus to modify the presentation of ourselves depending on what the particular role properly demands, and then hope we can get our inner states to go along for the ride—or at least not cause a crash—that each role takes us on. Some find in roles the villain that undermines authenticity; others might think there is no reason why a role cannot be any more or less authentic than a supposed true inner self might be.

In the last hundred years or so the issue of authenticity, named as such, became all the fashion so that we must either strive for it, or worry that it eludes us, or at least trick others, but mostly ourselves, that we have it. It came to be understood as an attribute of one's inner self and how it accords with one's words and deeds, a kind of deep sincerity of being. But it is not as if a similar matter of who or what you actually were, by some description, and whether you were true to it, did not exist before Sartre (and the nineteenth-century Romantics).[1] During the religious wars, whether you were a Protestant or Catholic was a matter of life and death, as were, at other times, whether you were an authentic Christian or a heretic.[2] On a routine and mundane basis, the truth of whether you were a coward or not, good for a loan or not, a good credit risk or not, was surely more crucial than just about anything in determining who or what you really were in more than a few social and moral domains. The issue had yet to become nine-tenths self-indulgent and self-congratulatory. Not even some of those who worried about whether they were saved or damned could match the narcissism, or plain old vulgar selfishness, of the modern quest for personal authenticity.

Matters of true identity—a kind of authenticity of a sort, though not the modern kind, that the person before you is whom he professes to be—is a frequent theme of trickster tales from the earliest of times. The standard plots of so much ancient comedy deal with doubling, mistaken identity, out and out cons, where every appearance of the usual or the normal should put you on the alert that you are about to be swindled or made a fool of. Yet, it was not as if identity and authenticity in nearly the modern sense were not engaged in some *pas de deux* centuries or millennia ago. When a certain Saul finds his inner being, his very soul, truer if he changes his name to Paul to move both up and out in his world, thereby transforming the world as much as himself, are we to believe his inner turmoil is somehow less reflective or reflexive than your average humanities professor's or psychotherapist's? Is the fronting of the issue of authenticity now nine parts a symptom of despair, demoralization at the inescapability of pretense in all this interiority, as in more religious times you found it hard not to suspect displays of piety as hypocritical, not least your own, that is, if you were being honest with yourself, which may or may not be part of what it also means to be true to yourself?[3]

I am fairly dubious about discourses of authenticity. So many claims of authenticity are pretenses, and the wise person should apply a steep discount to any claim of it, certainly if self-conferred. I most certainly accept the usefulness of the concept when it is deployed in narrow domains, for instance, whether that painting is an authentic Vermeer or whether that is an authentic legal document (its earliest sense in English). But the abstract noun *authenticity* seems pretty near vacuous to me, whereas the adjective *authentic* need not be, though we hardly blink at the phrase *authentic reproduction*.[4] It just might be that the fairly cogent idea of a fraud or a fake provides the foundation for, or is the very generator of, the much more elusive idea of authenticity.

Let's start with some very early matters of anxiety about what we might call authenticity, though not presented in quite that form. You would think the God of the Hebrew Bible would have no anxieties about his own authenticity as it relates especially to his identity, if we could hold him accountable for having to answer to our concepts rather than to his own. But he seems to be begging for us to test him on some of these matters. If in Genesis there is some doubt as to whether the God of Abraham is the same as the God of Isaac or the God of Jacob, that is fairly well settled by that book's end. But Exodus still does not present a God wholly secure as to who he is. His Oneness only becomes the chief attribute of his identity in Deuteronomy, before Christianity fractured him into three.

In Exodus 3.13 Moses asks God for his name so he can tell the Israelites who exactly is sending him (Moses) to lead them out of Egypt. God tells Moses to say to the people that "I Am That I Am" sent him (Exod. 3.14). God is playing games with his name, if we assume him to have a name before this moment of being asked to name himself. Though standard English translations of the Bible prefer the present tense ("I Am That I Am"), the Hebrew imperfect of God's answer is generally translated as a future tense—"I Will Be Who (or What) I Will Be"—which results in a dramatic shift in meaning as to the kind of character God is claiming to be. Luther employs the future: Gott sprach zu Mose: "ich werde sein, der ich sein werde" ("I will be who I will be"),[5] thus presenting us with a God who takes his essence to be manifested in arbitrariness, and moreover in a particular type of arbitrariness about his own identity and continuity of character, claiming for himself an infinite right and power to be a shapeshifter, all signs and wonders, masks and veils, storm clouds and pillars of fire, or still small voices. And his name? YHWH: strangely, it is a form of the verb *to be*. The future tense translation seems better to accord with the riddling way God chooses to name himself. He obviously means to riddle. Ultimately, any god worth his hire has to be something of a shapeshifter, such as Odin, or as that triune Christian God, now man, now God, now a dove, now one, now three, now three in one. The gods, in most mythologies I am familiar with, are shapeshifters. Theirs is partly the authenticity of the Trickster, and why should this God who names himself "I Will Be What I Will Be" be any different?

If the gods are projections of our own desires and anxieties, then it should be no great wonder that God is confused as to who he is or what it means to be true to himself—maybe even more confused than we are. At least you and I are locked into a fairly identifiable and continuous body, the template remaining stable even as almost all the cells and molecules have been exchanged several times during our lifetimes. But how was anyone to recognize that body as yours outside your village before there were photographs? Medievalists are always aware that people, even discounting for the inevitable cons, could not take any claimed identity for granted, as when exchanging hostages, for instance. But God or the gods did not have any identifiable single body. If they had a body at all, it had generally to be borrowed for the occasion. They also often appear as disembodied voices, or gusts of wind. A detached voice always raised issues of authenticity, as to who owned the voice and where it originated, whether it was heard properly, or whether it was not just a phantasm of the hearer, raising an issue for his, as well as the voice's, authenticity.

Just let me mention without even daring to unravel the messy issues that prophecy raises. Is a claimed prophecy true or false? Is the prophet true or false independent of the truth or falsity of his prophecy? God can choose the strangest of vehicles for his mouthpieces, not just official guys like Isaiah or Amos but also the crazy man on the street corner or a talking ass can be the vehicle of authentic prophecy as well.[6] Moreover, prophets often speak in gibberish: an animal appearing in a dream is last of all a lion or just a cigar; he stands for something else that requires interpretation. So it comes down to battles of which interpretations achieve recognition as providing the true key to the elusive meaning of the message, and that can toss us into the world of politics, where the king will have an array of official omen readers and interpreters to offer up their readings. Then too: an authentic prophet might also think himself privileged to engage in pious frauds. Part of the job of the authoritative prophet may be to substitute his own voice to say what he thinks God should want him to say even if his dream had God saying something else: a whole lot of (pious) faking going on.

Therein lies another mystery surrounding authenticity. It is one thing to *be* authentic; it is another matter to be recognized as such. The authentic must sell itself as authentic no less than the fake must sell itself as authentic. As briefly mentioned earlier (p. 85), truth no less than falsehood has to convince people of its truthfulness, and the moves are the same for both, unless, that is, authenticity at its core delights in its own rejection. If the person of average human intelligence (not a demanding standard, crows and octopi might exceed it) believes that you are the real thing, is that not pretty good proof you are not? Zarathustra up in Sils Maria would have thought so, as would many a self-conscious avant-gardiste. Did God himself or Jesus have doubts on this score?

Who makes the call regarding the authentic? We are not well positioned to make the call for ourselves with reliable accuracy; we tend to be too generous when evaluating ourselves. La Rochefoucauld nails it: "Our enemies get closer to the truth in their judgments of us than we get ourselves" (Maxim 458). Do we appoint some review board of, God forbid, therapists? But review boards, medal-awarding authorities and the like, are notoriously biased, if not corrupt. This theme makes for grand beginnings. It is the start point of the *Iliad*, even of the Bible. Cain kills Abel, not quite unreasonably thinking that God was playing favorites when he accepted Abel's offering but not his own. Says Mathilde de la Mole in *The Red and the Black*: "I can see nothing conferring honor . . . except a sentence of death. It's the only thing that can't be bought."[7] So Julien Sorel, that peasant conman extraordinaire, is the only man who meets her standard of real manhood. His whole story is one of sublime inauthenticity, as he loathes the corrupt layer upon layer of falsity that is restoration France, and sneers at its falseness because he is so much better at falseness than any of his contemporaries, a kind of Rameau's nephew. (So we arrive at the cheap observation that we can contemplate such a thing as authentic inauthenticity.)

Authenticity, if it is a virtue, is equally serviceable to moral defectives as to saints. Take the *poète maudit*, one of the more irritating of self-aggrandizing pretenses the nineteenth and early twentieth century came up with, much the same as authentic performance art is today. Orwell showed no mercy to the authenticity of the 'dead-endism' that struck the undergrad of the 1960s as powerfully profound:

> 'Disillusionment' was all the fashion. Everyone with a safe £500 a year turned highbrow and began training himself in *taedium vitae*. It was an age of eagles and of crumpets, facile despairs, backyard Hamlets, cheap return tickets to the end of the night.[8]

(I would give ten years of my life, especially if they are the ones from eighty to ninety, to write a passage like that, even granting the high likelihood that it is my own down-in-the-dumpsism that Orwell is sneering at.)

Measure the phoniness at the core of the romantic notions of the artist, or of Blut und Boden, or of Brook Farm or any hippy commune, all meant to strip away pretense as their first order of business. The inauthenticities of movements dedicated to seeking authenticity generated new hypocrisies and phoniness that made the old hypocrisies of false piety look respectable.

I must confess this: when it comes to pathetic pretentiousness, no Parisian avant-gardiste, no *poète maudit* could outdo me in June 1969 reading the Comte de Lautréamont's *Les Chants de Maldoror* (1868), in French no less, while on a bus loaded with young boys/men heading down from Green Bay to the Milwaukee induction center for our draft physical as a preliminary to being shipped off to Vietnam. I had just graduated from college (the draft notice beat my diploma home by a week); the other eighty or so had mostly finished high school if that. The army discovered I had a slipped disc, two it turned out; thus, I avoided death in the jungle along with one overweight Oneida Indian, but how I managed to avoid being rightly murdered on that bus still mystifies me.

Industrialization and romanticism raised new anxieties about the real, the true. Mass production, political democracy, and fears of tawdry cheap knockoffs sent some to the faux authenticity of Walden Pond, others later to celebrating the machine, on the right as Futurists, on the left as five-year plans with fake factory output numbers (and mass dislocations of soon to be "dead souls"). Unique selves? What of your very self being mass-produced, let alone mass-murdered? Not only artworks can be reproduced and printed to hang in the dorms of university students but you also find you yourself duplicated, when you go to a football game or attend a demonstration or an academic conference, to say nothing of what the internet and social media platforms have done for mass replication of images of our unique and very authentic Photoshopped selves.

The previous paragraph, graced with nary an original thought, could pass for a screed written by a true believer in authenticity demoralized by the triumph of the inauthentic. Yet it works equally for a nonbeliever in the authentic self to mock the idea of lamenting its imagined disappearance. As I have said, it is very hard to separate claims of authenticity from pretense, from fakery and self-indulgence.

Those who sing the praises of authenticity, of being true to oneself, leave me cold. Return to that authentic 'self,' the very self Polonius, whom the exceedingly intelligent Hamlet thought an idiot, tells his son Laertes, who is an idiot, to be true to, neither father nor son to be trusted with giving sound advice or with taking it when given.[9] I have always thought that what Polonius really meant in his famous speech is to remind Laertes to stay within his budget. Nor is what is meant by the Delphic "Know Thyself" clear. Socrates keeps shifting his own sense of what it means. I always took it mainly to mean not to get too big for your breeches, so that it more accurately meant "Know Thy Place" or "Know Thy League," and basically restates what I understand Polonius to be saying. Mostly though "Know Thyself" is yet another instance of the perversity of the oracle's sense of humor, in this case meaning to send you off in search of an interpretation that pleases you, which were to be had for a dime a dozen. For a higher price you could bribe the Pithia herself.[10]

Authenticity? True to myself? What if I am good enough at some roles to qualify as the genuine article but am pretty much a fraud or merely incompetent at others? Is it only the roles I am good at for which I can claim authenticity? Or is being good at the role exactly what we expect of the able conman? Do I get credit for being fully authentic if I own up to being four-fifths a fraud or an incompetent? Or do I only get credit if I determine to improve the four-fifths of me that is a sham? I leave aside the whole issue of the status of *training* to be authentic, except to ask this: Is it something one can train for, or is one merely blessed with it? If you have to work for it, can it ever be a goal you strive for directly without undoing the very possibility of attaining it, as in the command "be spontaneous" or "be surprised"? Or must you achieve it without striving for it at all but get there by indirection, unless, that is, you were born to it?

The psychobabble regarding self-realization and authenticity assumes an ultimate unity of self. I want to agree. Surely I am more than the collection of actors in the play that bears my name and inhabits my body. But I do not feel myself to be the director of that play either, for

I am hardly calling all the shots. I mostly feel like I am a bit player in other people's plays, mouthing scripts that I have not composed, like Stoppard's Rosencrantz or Guildenstern.[11] Worse is that not only am I acting a part I often did not write but I am also either seated in the audience for the performance or, as in the case of that All Souls' incident where the me observing me had been blinded by drink, I am then treated to cuing up and playing the recorded performance at 3 AM.

Grimly: I know when I am at one with the real me: it is when I want to disappear in shame, usually at 3 AM, alone, with a very queasy stomach. That is the only moment, exposed and overcome with shame, in which I am completely stripped of the veils and costumes of the roles I am forced to play.[12] Pure unaccommodated me. Wouldn't you know that such a stripping took place in the bright light of 4 PM, the afternoon sun streaming through the windows, in the Q and A after the talk that was the first iteration of this chapter?

II.

The next few sentences may seem non sequitur, but there is a method to letting them serve as an introduction to a new theme. I have wondered, even before puberty, at the infinitude of hatred a Jew is born to and the self-hatred that seems to be the hallmark of so much diasporan Jewish identity. Even now when trying to account for the singularity, vehemence, depth, and ineradicability of anti-Semitism, I get something akin to that dizzying feeling one gets looking up at the stars on a clear winter night out in the country away from light pollution, but that is a dizziness prompted by a glimpse of infinitude at its most splendid, while contemplating the infinitude of anti-Semitism changes the valence of my dizziness, but the dizziness is still identifiably of the kind one experiences facing Infinity. Rather than overcome by splendor, I sink into confused despair that my pretense of misanthropy should not resolve itself into sincerely held Swiftian thoughts of eliminating the Yahoos from the face of the earth.

I suppose it should be considered a cheap move on my part to have made the claim I am about to make in Germany, when, if I had guts, I would do it in Hungary, Poland (if ever invited to these places), England (especially before a convocation of Laborites), or in many parts of my own country, but saying this in a cultural studies conference anywhere in the West would do as well.

Here is the claim, somewhat whacky, but hear me out. Could it be that from about the thirteenth century on the core naked Western authentic self housed a certain indelible identity: a Jew at its core, whether you were a Jew or not? Could it not be claimed that the authentic Christian self is, in more senses than one, Jewish? Let me try to get at this thought experiment (it is not really defensible as more than as an experiment) this way.

Freud in his *Der Witz und seine Beziehung zum Unbewußten* tells a joke (ask yourself why I am giving the German title of *Jokes and Their Relation to the Unconscious* when I obviously read it in English translation, which will be the cause of my public stripping, tarring, and feathering):

> A doctor, who had been asked to look after the Baroness at her confinement, pronounced that the moment had not come, and suggested to the Baron that in the meantime they should have a game of cards in the next room. After a while a cry of pain from the Baroness struck the ears of the two men: "Ah, mon Dieu, que je souffre!" Her husband sprang up, but the doctor signed to him to sit down: "It's nothing. Let's go on with the game!" A little later there were again sounds from the pregnant woman: "Mein Gott, mein Gott, what terrible pains!"—"Aren't you going in, Professor?" asked the Baron.—"No, no. It's not time yet." At last there came from next door an unmistakable cry of "Ai, waih, waih!" The doctor threw down his cards and exclaimed: "*Now* it's time."[13]

The point of the joke is that for the Baroness, an assimilated Jew, each increase in pain strips away the most recent accretion in the process of assimilation, the *Drang nach Westen* (the push westward) of the emancipated Jew. She is still able to maintain her role as a French-speaking German *haute bourgeoise* qua aristocrat in the midst of minor pain. Jack up the pain and she starts drifting eastward back across the Rhine to *echt* (pure) German, until agony rips off this last mask to reveal the inescapable Jew east of the Vistula. The pain of intense labor strips away the layers of inauthenticity revealing the ineradicable Jew as her true self.

Now for my confession. In the talk in Freiburg I reproduced a discussion of this joke that I had already published in *Faking It*, but, as I already mentioned, I got caught out by a conference participant. I have already emended the last cry of the Baroness in Freud's joke; that is not how I presented it in my talk. There and in *Faking It* I quoted it as it appears in the Standard Edition of Freud's works edited and mostly translated by James Strachey. Strachey did not render her last cry of pain as "Ai, waih, waih!," which is the way Freud had it in the German text and as I now quoted it, but as "Aa-ee, aa-ee, aa-ee!"

I called Freud out for bowdlerizing what obviously had to be something like "oy vey" as the Baroness's last cry. I blamed him for rendering the Yiddish the joke required into a primal scream, "Aa-ee," not identifiable as Yiddish. I accused him of trying to make the obviously Jew joke 'pass' as she had been trying to do until that moment.[14] But her scream was not an inarticulate prelinguistic primal scream. As the conference participant informed me coldly, the "Ai, waih, waih" of the German text was an attempt to render the Galician Jewish dialect, and that it was thus sinking the Baroness even lower than proper Yiddish would have done to the lowest of the Ostjuden in the standard internal status rankings that Jews constructed for themselves (obviously disputed by Galizianers). As the Strachey translation has it, it still is largely a Jew joke, but very unfunny because the last line just sinks into foul misogyny, instead of a modestly entertaining example of emancipated Jewish self-hatred, knowing that no matter how much civilization they/we acquire, no matter how much artistic and scientific achievement, at their/our core is the sidelocked, caftaned, fish-belly pale-skinned, unattractive, and unphysical Talmud student (Jewish women were more flatteringly viewed, if they passed certain physical criteria, as exotically alluring; it is a Jewish woman in the joke who had managed, it seems, to have married up, unless her husband is also a Jew that had climbed up).

But what I took to be the bowdlerization set me off on hostile speculations, and now that I see them in front of me, I cannot believe how much I forced the bowdlerized joke to do some dirty work it was not up to. Still I present it, because though my reading of the joke may not be remotely justifiable, the claims I used it as an excuse to make still provide some small snack for thought. Here it is: What the inaccurate

English translation had done by de-Judaicizing such an obvious Jew joke was to generate a perverse deeper Judaicizing joke. What it revealed, I claimed to my present dismay, was the denial Christians must engage in to blind themselves to the Jew at their core.[15] Even the Jew-speaking Mary must have screamed out some kind of Jew talk in this most moving moment of human life, when she gave birth to her Holy Jewish Child. So the authentic Christian is what, then? A Jew at his core, with a better hairdo. I suppose I was trying to make my German audience feel uncomfortable for the crimes of their grandparents, but I failed miserably. The Germans got me. What else is new? I knew also that this interpretation was really a real reach, and my motive, not very pure, was to take a kind of cowardly revenge of pure *ressentiment,* in Nietzsche's sense, against Germans, who have established, thanks to the misbehavior of their grandparents, the most moral of Western polities.

But here I was suggesting the deep inauthenticity of a Christian denying he was a Jew at his core, his Christian identity utterly subsumed into, as well as having emanated from, its Jewish parentage, and I ended up instead revealing myself an inauthentic scholar, not having even bothered to check the original. I became enmeshed in the emanations of a joke that turned out to be at my expense, and I was the unwitting teller of it. I was passing as a scholar, intoning on a German text (written by a Jew) that I was taking cheap shots at, but in an English translation that had hung me out before an audience of Germans, in a talk on authenticity no less. Oy vey iz mir. Embarrassed? Ashamed? I apologized. My ears were so red hot I thought they would burst into flames (Was my face as red? Did I want to vomit?). Rare as it is for apologies to be sincere, this time I can vouch that mine was; the sincerity was in my blood-red ears, a perfectly authentic apology. What was I to do? I confessed error, made no excuses, thanked him, and made some attempt at humor by claiming it was rare to come away from an academic conference having learned anything at all, but I sure had been taught a lesson at this one.

What put the questioner on to me? I do not believe he knew Freud's book by heart or even recalled that joke, but he did not like what I was doing with the joke's last line, generalizing from what I mistakenly took as a bowdlerization that suppressed the necessary Yiddish of the joke into an attempt to render the questioner and the rest of the audience into self-hating Jews at their inauthentic Christian cores. So he reaches for his laptop and searches Projekt Gutenberg (Projekt fitting more naturally with Gutenberg than Project) and there it was.[16] Suppose I had done my homework authentically? My German is such that it would have taken me about three weeks looking up a lot of words to read *Der Witz und seine Beziehung zum Unbewußten*, though that is no excuse, for it would have taken me only about three minutes to read the joke in German. But even had I done so I would not have understood that the last line was an attempt to mimic the Galizianer dialect. In my defense, I think I would at least have known that *waih* was *veh*, *weh*: Old Norse *vei*, and English *woe*, and not Strachey's "aa, ee," not a preverbal primal scream.

I, of course, gave the talk in English, as did all the other speakers, only one other of whom had English as their mother tongue. I cannot hide, if not quite my shame, then surely my embarrassment, that when I am in Germany or in the Nordic countries I am incapable of following the maxim "when in Rome . . ." Out of some kind of guilty accommodation I try to speak clearly and slowly with no nonstandard idioms and make an apology at the start about my northern Wisconsin accent whose ugliness is almost without rival outside of Boston or Queens. But just imagine the contempt my corrector must have had for me, not unjustly.

Thus chastened, let me still maintain, sans Freud's joke, something about authenticity and the fraught problem of the Jew in the Diaspora (though the black-hatted orthodox seem to be immune to self-hate, certain as they are of their divine election). Among the many hypotheses offered to explain anti-Semitism, at least in part, has been a supposed Christian envy of the Jews for having been chosen as God's people (Deut. 14.2), whatever this might involve, whether, for instance, such election was transferable, as Paul suggested. There is, however, no ambiguity in God having chosen Hebrew as his native language, the language in which to issue his commands, demands, and promises. This view would then propose that a Christian could resolve the pain of his envy by making the lot of the Jew unenviable—make it so unpleasant as to let Christians breathe a sigh of relief that God had not chosen Christians in this cursed way. They would instead seek to make the one in one hundred odds of my being born a Jew a matter of having been 'selected' rather than chosen.

Imagine, though, how to explain that God became man as a Jew rather than, say, as a Greek or a Roman. You could argue that God chose the most humiliating way to humble himself, even back then. A Jew as the most authentic human? Impossible. But should God have been incarnated as Caesar or Socrates or Alexander, rather than as a Galilean Jew, his incarnation would carry a very different message, for those guys were too heroic to be authentically human. They were not sufficiently debased, even though Socrates was in some respects crucified and ugly as sin. You would never dare pin a yellow star on them, as most certainly would have been pinned on Jesus were he to have chosen his Second Coming in any number of European cities in any number of centuries (is the 'jaundice' of this chapter's title an unconscious pinning of that star on myself?).

God, like pagan deities, as I have already noted, cannot seem to shake an attraction to tricksterism; there are more than a few ironies in choosing to enflesh himself as a poor Jew. Can we suppose a deep Christian anxiety that God, instead of masking himself as the Jew Jesus was, in fact, stripping himself of all his own veils and masks, revealing the naked truth about his own identity? It turns out God's indelible Hebrew-speaking self, in the Christian exegetical tradition—or at least the view that won out—his core, is the Jew Jesus (as the Son, as the Logos), who is harbored deep within his bosom, and surely coeternal and equal to him, lest you be declared an Arian heretic like so many of the early Germanic Volk, until the time was ripe to loose the Son upon the world in the first decades of the Roman Empire.[17]

For the anti-Semite, and perhaps for Freud, the Jew has a fixed self beneath his masks. It is Western civilizing Christian culture that provides the veils of roles and poses, fronts and fakes, but it succeeded in making the Jew immutable and necessary. Just where would Hungarian and Polish nationalism be for the last 150 years without the idea of the Jew, which hardly needs any living ones to work its wonder?[18] If there were no Jews in the picture Kurds would swap places with Palestinians as the chief objects of solicitude on university campuses in the United Kingdom, European Union, and United States. Want to unite Europe, East and West, North and South, across the Slavic/Germanic/Romance divides, across the Catholic/Protestant divide? Jew hating is more durable than a common market, a common currency. It is the one card European Muslims play with more than sufficient energy to make their own fraught case for fitting in. And though Europe hates them, it does not find a Muslim seated inside at the core of their authentic selves, even though such would indeed be the case for many a Spaniard or Portuguese, in whose souls (and blood) Jew and Muslim miraculously exist side by side in relative peace.

The Jew does not quite figure in this way in America, for in the United States the Jew is only an obsession of the real nut jobs, though there is no shortage of these lunatics (and they are all well armed to boot). The American core denied identity is more Black than it is Jewish, so that America was the one country where a Jew could actually live a better life than he or she could live anywhere ever. This was hardly a gift from the Blacks, who surely had no wish to give it, but arguably it is on their backs that Jews could live somewhat less anxiously in America than anywhere else.

In my disgust book I noted the thought experiment of a prominent researcher on disgust who asked us to consider the effects on a barrel of wine of adding a tablespoon of raw sewage to it compared with the effects on a barrel of raw sewage of adding a tablespoon of the finest wine to it.[19] The wine is immediately transformed by the sewage, rendered disgusting and undrinkable. The sewage, however, remains just what it is despite the addition of the wine. The sewage has a durable essence, call it authenticity if you wish, that is easy to create and preserve, but the wine? Whatever authenticity it can claim is ever so fragile and vulnerable. Pollutants are powerful in a way that purifying agents are not, the good again outmanned and outgunned by the bad. The deck is stacked in favor of degradation by the low as against elevation by the high.[20] Purifying agents give themselves up in the process of purification in a kind of suicide mission, like the soap that is rinsed away in a mutual scummy embrace with dirt, going down the drain together, so that we can declare ourselves fresh and clean. But a pollutant infiltrates, thrives, and multiplies, transforming what it comes into contact with into more pollutant. How can any authenticity survive the ineffable transformative power of the Polluting, the most truly authentic power there is?

The power of the pollutant is the power of the Jew in the eyes of the anti-Semite. Take the case of medieval Spain, which cajoled, threatened, and forced its Jews to convert during the fourteenth and fifteenth centuries, finally expelling those who remained in 1492.[21] Judenrein, right? Then the anxieties set in. What if these Conversos really were Jews in secret? They are passing for Christians and marrying our daughters and sons, and we marry theirs. And handy-dandy who is a Jew, who a Christian?

The end, in a kind of poetic justice, was that instead of making Jews into Christians as they had intended, Christians feared and believed that they were being turned into Jews. One drop of blood did you in. The proof of Converso falsity? They appeared to be Christian, and that was exactly the appearance that could no longer be trusted, for wouldn't it be like a false Jew to counterfeit his Christianity, like the Devil with his superb command of Holy Writ? So the most damning appearances were precisely those that looked perfectly fine.[22] There was nothing more suspiciously inauthentic than looking, being, and acting Christian. Christians had turned themselves into acting Christians.

The anxiety was ratified and confirmed well into the twentieth century. Under its entry for the Grand Inquisitor Tómas de Torquemada, *The Catholic Encyclopedia* (1913 edition) reasserts a view that contributed nonnegligibly to the destruction of European Jewry within three decades of that edition's appearance:

> At that time the purity of the Catholic Faith in Spain was in great danger from the numerous Marranos and Moriscos, who, for material considerations, became sham converts from Judaism and Mohammedanism to Christianity. The Marranos committed serious outrages against Christianity and endeavoured to judaize the whole of Spain.[23]

The Jew? He was authenticity itself, the pure power of Pollution, and though perhaps baptismal water might clean a Jew up on occasion, that did not sway Himmler, and now with our genome readily available two different genetic services peg me as 98.7% Ashkenazi Jew. But that kind of near 'purity of sangre' is nothing to celebrate, and probably only possible elsewhere on some remote Polynesian island or in some

inaccessible Himalayan mountain valley. Mine is a function of ghet-
toization, the Pale of Settlement, and several centuries of lockup and
lockdown. But if Christians were getting to us with firebrands, nooses,
defenestrations, rapes, eviscerations by rape, and bludgeons, that does
not mean we were not getting to them in secret, or so they feared. In
the good old United States it was all out in the open: my two sisters and
I married Roman Catholics. Go figure.[24] But our kids would still go up
the chimney, even if they come in at only 49.4% corrupt.

7

Lord of the Table: Judges 19 and the Last Supper

THIS CHAPTER, LIKE THE preceding one, requires an account of its origins. I was invited to speak to an audience of scientists, nutritionists, and their students at the University of Missouri in 2012 for their Sciences and Society Program's annual symposium. The titled theme that year was "Food Sense." I figured that they intended the quasi-rhyme or visual pun on food and good; 'food sense' was meant to invite the next letter of the alphabet to follow and, by unconscious suggestion, lead to 'good sense.' But then I wondered why food and good did not perfectly rhyme like good and hood or food and mood, and I got myself into a regular depression as to whether I once knew this or never knew it but thought I had, for more than forty years ago I taught history of the English language and would or should have known the answer.

I discovered some time later, to my horror, that the talk had been posted on YouTube, a permission I would have refused had I been asked. Most likely, it had been asked in fine print, which, even though I have a law degree and teach in a law school, I never can get myself to read it in the many documents I have signed over my lifetime. I do not advise my students, many of whom will spend a good part of their working lives composing fine print, to do as I do, or rather to do as I don't do.[1]

Bear with the somewhat strange course this chapter takes; recall that its origins lie in eating and it roams widely. If the chapter makes a contribution to scholarship, it is in its reading of the Last Supper together with Judges 19. What goes before, the bulk of the exposition, can be understood as setting the table for that supper.

Suppose you, a medievalist, could magically time-travel back to a feast in a farmhouse or castle among the people you have spent your professional life studying. What would that first hour be like? Would your reading knowledge of their language give you a clue as to what was being said before you had another several months to adjust? What mortifications might you suffer from seeing that you had gotten more than a few things wrong, that, like so much work in certain suspect academic disciplines for which you had never disguised your contempt, you had propagated more error than truth, more darkness than light?

What about the smells, of the people in particular, their bodies and their breath? Will the air be so rank and odors far too strongly unpleasant to be masked by the smoke of the burning peat (assuming we are in Iceland), the dense smoke helping to keep the ubiquitous lice under small control? Within days you can add chilblains to the discomfort of the itching. More than a few of you, unless ardent campers and hikers, would refuse the trip outright if you could not bring sufficient toilet paper for the duration.

The concerns I am now raising pretty much capture the difference of what it means to be a medieval historian rather than an anthropologist. We enjoy a substantial benefit in not having to deal face to face with our subjects on their turf. I might love *reading* how Egill Skallagrímsson behaved at feasts, he tickling me and my students to no end, but I sure would not want to be drinking *with* him, lest he take offense at something I did or said, or did not do or say, and gouge my eye out, purposely vomit all over me, or knife me in the gut.[2]

Remember it is a feast we are at. Look around, observe how they eat, what constitutes proper table manners, even if you, against all your historical commitments, think at first that they have none worth the name. You know you would be wrong, for little is more highly regulated than eating in company, probably more then than now; just sitting in the wrong seat could get you beaten, even killed, as I have already had occasion to note in this book. And you had better find the food edible if not good, and praiseworthy in either case, even if the meat is rather high or, in the opposite vein, if you, the animal lover, had seen the meat was very fresh because three lambs had had their throats slit right before your eyes, gutted, flayed, parted, and tossed in the pot.

It requires no historical learning to understand that it would give offense not to eat what was offered. That might pass for as universal a custom as there is, with cultures varying only on how the game of offer and polite refusal and reoffer is played. You remind yourself that you demanded that your students in the rich West try to imagine what scarcity—serious scarcity—of calories and of affordable clothing to keep the body heat in meant, except for the few rich or those lucky enough, such as the natives of the Pacific Northwest, to live where nature was bountiful. We have found in our sybaritic culture that plentiful food does not mean we are that much less obsessed with it than when you never knew whether you would have any tomorrow and often wouldn't by the time spring rolled around. We too count calories, though for rather different reasons than the reason they counted them, and we too imbue food with moral qualities depending on its source and how it was procured, whether, in effect, the proper blessings were said.

My implicit suggestion is that disgust would figure largely in getting acclimated; but fear may loom larger. Remember these are the people whose violence and edgy wit you love to write about. Although you wondered if at times you may have played up the threat in the air because it made more interesting copy, you, even at *their* most peaceful, know you are no match for the least of them (especially the women), being as you are an academic, thereby numbering yourself among the least martial and most cowardly of professions. Fear is remarkable for displacing the experience of other sentiments that might be trying to make themselves felt, such as wonder, interest, the feeling of the luck at having all this firsthand information at your disposal, and the delight, or rather the relief, that you got some things right.[3] Of a sudden someone laughs at you and launches a lamb shank or singed sheep's head in your direction, all in good fun, I suppose, but others join in and you pray for aid to St. Ælfheah, Archbishop of Canterbury (d. 1012), the patron saint of those who are 'boned' to death in this fashion at a Scandinavian feast. At the point of death by the bones launched at him, Ælfheah was finished off with an axe to the skull. It is said that the Danes were angry with him for his refusing to let himself be ransomed.[4] Bone throwing of this sort was not just a party game (a version of it figures in the death of

Baldr in that well-known myth), but it also figured as a legal sanction in the Danish law governing the king's retainers. A retainer who was persistent in violating the rules of the hall "and . . . refuses to come to his senses, they decreed that he should be seated last of all, *and pelted with bones at any man's pleasure.*"[5]

This prologue is a way of indicating my own fear that some of my topic may offend, for it will eventually touch on the Eucharist, especially the first one at the Last Supper, interpretations of which I am aware have led to the deaths of hundreds of thousands and the destruction of whole polities. The topic, broadly construed, is about the obligation-creating power of giving and receiving food, of cutting it up for distribution: contract formation of a sort at its most rawly foundational.[6]

I.

Food can make you fat; and it can also make you friends and foes. We signal sociability, kinship and friendship, the existence of peace and truce by eating or drinking together. Eating alone, especially in a restaurant, is a classic image of despair. When relegated to it, you pretend to be grading papers or reading serious matter as a form of justification. This is probably the only true virtue of smartphones: it gives you something to do when exposed as being very alone, a proto-pariah, amidst what seem to you to be convivial others.

We all know that to be invited to someone's for dinner obliges us to make a return in kind at some later date, or to forfend that unpleasant obligation we might try to satisfy it up front by bringing a bottle of wine a little pricier than usual and noticeably so, though not so gauchely as to leave the price sticker on. We are made debtors by the invitation. This of course was well known long before Marcel Mauss theorized it. Every gift demands its return, Odin says.[7]

Consider now two laws, one Frankish, the other Norwegian. A provision in the Frankish Salic law (parts are as early as the sixth century CE) sets forth a ritual necessary to conclude an adoption, to graft someone into one's kin. First, the adopter is to toss a stick (*festuca*) in the lap of the adoptee: this is a public gesture symbolizing the intent to transfer property rights to the adoptee. But that is only step one of the ritual. To complete the adoption, you, the person being adopted, had to have witnesses testify that you "assembled three or more guests and fed them, and these three or more guests offered thanks to you in accepting the food and ate porridge (*pultes*, i.e., basic symbolic food) at your table."[8] Until you fed guests, such that you are clearly seen to be the source of the food and thus have imposed on them the obligation to thank you, you are not in full control of the property that has been given you by the ceremony of the stick. You had to show you had exercised the ability and the power to give a carrot for that stick, and thus to oblige others by your giving. That feeding was the sign that it was now really *your* property.

Second law. In the Frostathing law of twelfth-century Norway an illegitimate child can be "led into the kin" and thus become capable of inheriting if the heirs consent and if the father gives a feast supplied with ale brewed from at a minimum three *sáld*s of malt (about nine bushels).[9] Here the expense at the front end is all the adopter's (at the back end his legitimate children have just seen the denominator on their share of the patrimony increased, and thus their share decreased).

This ceremony adds to the symbolism of shared drinking a requirement that a three-year-old ox be slaughtered, which no doubt will be served up for food, but the ox's specific role in this ritual is to provide the hide cut from its rear right leg from which a shoe is to be fashioned. That shoe is to be worn first by the adoptee and then passed on to be put on by the father's legitimate sons who are already of age. All are to step into the same skin. His minor sons are excused from wearing the shoe, but they must sit on their father's knee, he thereby locking in their consent. We will return to this ritual amalgam of eating, drinking, and butchering, the slicing and dicing of flesh, as well as shares of a patrimony, when we get to Judges and Jesus.

The Salic and Frostathing adoptions track in a small way another form of adoption, the adoption of your own *legitimate* child, for it too requires adoption of a sort when infanticide was an allowable option. For a newborn to qualify as an heir—in Iceland now—not only must it have been born alive and of a mother who was bought with a bride price of more than a mark and who was wedded and brought to bed before witnesses, but also "food had to come into its mouth" (*Grágás* Ia 222). The baby is not fully admitted into the family until then, and even Christianity does not fully humanize a baby until it has been baptized. Should the infant die before it was baptized, it is to be buried in that bleak no-man's land, along with outlaws and others not entitled to proper church burial, outside hallowed ground in a grim Limbo on earth (Ia 12).

Being given and consuming food is crucial to make an heir, food being in one sense the platonic form of what property was, not land, which was mostly only of use to the extent it generated food. This first taste of food is the first taking in by the child of the family's wherewithal, and it means the baby now bears rights.

The legality of infanticide before Christianity forbade it in the Northlands meant that getting born required a decision to be made whether there were sufficient resources to raise the child up.[10] Among us in the rich West, human young are near useless, and especially those of the educated classes, until they reach about twenty-eight, if then. In a sheep-herding society like saga Iceland, and lucky for them, a child could start earning much of its keep as early as age seven, but by then the parents were likely to have already had many children who had died at one, two, three, four, and five, so that in order to get one child to seven you had to invest about as much as we do to get one healthy useless child to twenty-eight (there might be a universal constant of the uselessness of children, independent of culture and mortality rates, twenty-eight years or thereabouts; for us it takes one child, for them anywhere between three and nine to get the total to twenty-eight years).[11] The ritual of inclusion, the ritual in which the head of household waived his right to expose the baby, often involved putting milk, water, or food on its lips. Such rituals made much of the symbolism of giving food, no less than did the Frankish adoption ceremony of which it was something of a cousin.[12]

Baptism, the general Christian ritual of inclusion, employs a different set of meanings drawing on symbols of purification. Judaism still gestures toward food, though quite obliquely, because meat figures in it, mostly by metaphor. Jewish boys get sliced and diced, a piece of flesh of the organ that is in a variety of languages euphemistically named 'meat' or in Middle and early Modern English 'flesh'[13] offered to God to seal and confirm the contract being made, much in the manner that in the ancient Mediterranean and Mesopotamian world contracts and treaties were sealed by the sacrifice of animals or, in one famous instance, by splitting edible animals between whose parts the party to be bound walked (see Gen. 15.8–17). And of course human blood would often do, since it required cutting flesh to draw it. Herodotus reports in a treaty between the Lydians and the Medes that both parties cut their forearms and licked the blood of the other (1.74).[14] This is all the stuff of nineteenth-century history of religion, of Genesis itself, and thus unlikely to be new or surprising.[15]

Shift now to a manumission ritual in Norway, the part of the ceremony the ex-slave is responsible for. To be fully counted among the free involves, in typical Nordic style, a drinking party. In the earliest Norwegian laws a freed slave or a freedman who seeks full freedom must brew and treat guests to 'freedom ale' (*frelsisöl*).[16] The quantity that must be brewed is specified, the amount yielded by three *sáld*s of malt at a minimum, and his master must be the guest of honor, given the high seat. To make sure the master is fully honored and to help make sure he can enjoy himself, the freedman must not invite any people with whom the master is involved in adversarial legal proceedings, which in some cases would severely limit the guest list. A woman must also conclude her manumission similarly, which leads to this grim law governing the marriage of two such freed people, perhaps bankrupted by funding all that drinking at their freedom feasts:

> if they come into dire straits then are their children grave-destined people (*grafgangsmenn*). A grave shall be dug in the churchyard and they are to be placed in it to die. The master shall take the one out who is the last survivor and feed him from then on.[17]

Since we are now among the dead, brief mention should also be made of 'grave ale,' which in some Nordic law was the drinking fete necessary for an otherwise qualified heir to take from his dead ancestor. It was to take place either on the seventh day or the thirtieth day in the Norwegian Gulathing law after the death, which gave it its name of the 'seventh' (*sjaund*)[18]—the text takes care to remind its readers or hearers that this ritual drinking is also called inheritance ale (*erfiöl*) or soul ale (*sáluöl*). This last name looks like a late attempt to patina a pagan funeral custom with some Christian veneering.[19] This ale feast has elaborate procedures set forth in another provision, for the seventh-day ale is also a debt court in which the claims against the decedent's estate are settled. Drinking apparently helps things along, but more obviously, sharing drink is the way a deal is sealed, claims heard and settled, and thus a clear and clean title can pass to the heir, who presides at the feast/court.[20]

So far this is pretty mild stuff, mostly feasts that are part of a legal ritual necessary to effect transfers of title or to alter an old status or confirm a new one—mild, that is, if we forget for a moment the lot of the *grafgangsmenn*, those children who lose that appalling game of "last kid breathing wins."

Now a law from Kent (c. 630 CE), in which the ritual aspects largely disappear and it is the mere eating or giving of hospitality that generates legal duties and liabilities all on its own: "if a man provides lodging for three nights to a trader, or someone who has come over the border, at his own home and feeds him, and that man does any harm to any-one, either he [the host] shall bring him to justice, or be liable for the wrongs himself."[21] Certain Icelandic laws raise a different issue: it was illegal to give certain people hospitality. If you fed a sturdy beggar, you were liable to what is known as lesser outlawry, three-year exile and loss of property. You had a defense if you could show that you only took in the wastrel to give him a sound whipping, and you could still offer that as a defense even if other householders joined in flogging him (a bit jaw-dropping that added proviso; *Grágás* Ib 179). A vagrant was not dealt with kindly in the Icelandic laws: you could castrate him for free, for if he happened to die from infection or bleeding out, you were im-mune from prosecution (Ib 203, II 151). It seems fairly clear from other provisions that the castration is not to punish him for his vagrancy but to prevent him from producing more hungry mouths to feed that he was in no position to support.[22]

Feeding someone makes him your own, adopts him in effect. But for how long? The Kentish provision surely makes you responsible after the three-day period if he stays on at your place. Should he kill someone on the fourth day the victim's kin could look to you for compensation. But suppose he kills someone three days after he leaves your place, or one month after? The matter is far from clear. I doubt that the moment he walks out your door you are free from liability. Your risk will fade

by degrees. You would unlikely be totally risk free until your obligation was intercepted by the next householder who hosted him for three
days. Even then your liability would linger if when he left your place
you knew of his intention to kill or steal, or reasonably should have
known. This is a topic for another day. But add this datum: in Iceland if
another person's dog happened to be tagging along after you suspecting
you might give him a treat, and you did, then if the dog bit someone or
worried some sheep you were liable; you had to shoo him away (Ib 188).
Again, giving food bound someone to you as long as it was accepted,
and no dog I know is about to refuse a treat. The guest (human or ca-
nine), in other words, was grafted into your household, or onto your
legal person, whether you liked it or not, merely because you fed him.

No wonder there is so much fear of the guest, even today. They eat
you out of house and home and, in that world of scarce calories, could
thus eat you to death. This anxiety is captured in the etymology of the
word *guest*. The word *guest* is merely a different form of the word *host*.
Both come from the same Indo-European root and are merely different
phonological and semantic outcomes of that root. That same root gave
rise not only to the structural opposites of host and guest but also to the
moral opposites of hospitality and hostility. If that root kindly provided
places of respite like hotels and hospitals, on the darker side it produced
an armed host, a host of guests, which if uninvited is what a band of
raiders was, and they were hearty eaters, no differently than the people
you count as friends can be when you invite them over. Plug in today
your own anxiety when you hear a doorbell ring, even when you are
expecting company. The core sense of the word that generated all these
opposites appears to have been 'stranger.'[23]

A group of men is rarely a benign phenomenon, nor is, in the early
Germanic world, a solitary man, traveling alone, whose lack of accom-
paniment marked him, one feared, as either a thief or an outlaw, as
someone, that is, who could or had the option to operate 'in secret.'
Either way, as guests or a hostile band, a friend or a thief, these outsiders
threaten to exhaust your stores. You either made them welcome guests or
they made you a victim, like the sacrificial communion host.[24] The group
approaching your farm can surround your house and capture it, or you
can placate them by inviting them in; both are costly outcomes, but there
is something of a threat lurking in people showing up at your door: thus

the early root sense of the English word *threat*, which simply meant a band of men.[25] Under Hobbesian assumptions—to which we might add animal-behaviorist ones too—one of your fellow beings is before anything else a cause for concern, a danger, a threat. As a first-order matter, something, or someone, looking at you, fixing you with his/her/its eyes, usually means to make a meal of you or to make love to you, or if you are a female mantis eyeing her mate, both at once. And if humans are not really given to ingesting other humans, then another person is a threat to your flesh anyway, because he will make demands on your substance, your wherewithal, the very stuff that puts meat on your own bones.

A move in the Icelandic blood feud, called *dreita inni*, 'to make dirt inside' or 'to shit indoors,' involved a conscious parody of the rules of hospitality, before anyone knew of the etymological identity of hostility and hospitality. You surround the farm of your enemy for three days and block the doors so that the occupants of the household had no access to the privy outside, thereby making them have to befoul the indoors. There is nasty wit involved in the move, for the aggressor takes care to abide strictly (and thus, of course, ironically) by the three-day limit that custom imposes on the uninvited guest.[26] These 'guests' will not overstay their proper welcome. We have only one detailed description of the ritual;[27] other references tersely note it thus: "in that year X dreitr inni'd Y," showing we are dealing with a term of art that needs no further explication to contemporaries.

I am painting a rather dark picture; there are obviously brighter sides, and much simpler convivial and kindly hostings and guestings. For instance, the Icelandic laws envisage charitably taking someone in for "God's sake" and maintaining him when it is not your obligation to do so. Should that lucky recipient of your hospitality die and turn out to be solvent, you take ahead of his heirs. Thus, feeding this poor person ended up not with you adopting him, but him, after a fashion, adopting you. That is, any charitable outlay, a gift, can become a legally cognizable debt, a loan, and must be repaid ahead of any other claims.[28]

II.

Eating is subject to intense ritualization in just about every culture, as I said earlier. Eating together has an official starting point, whether it be merely 'sitting down to dinner' or, more formally, saying a prayer, or having the host break or carve a food that works as a metaphor for all food, such as bread does in many cultures, or meat in others.

I have already discussed the seating protocols and the anxieties it generated in chapter 3. But now we are all seated together, jovial companions, companion meaning literally the person you eat *panis* (i.e., bread) *com* (i.e., with), a word entering late Latin, it appears, as a calque of a Germanic word the Germans in the Roman army had for messmate.[29] Shift now our focus back on the host, the master of the table or of the benches, the lord of the hall.

Lord, the word, shows the erosion and shifting of sounds that cause languages to differentiate themselves from one another over time. Back in the year 600 the word that became our *lord* looked like this in Old English: *hláfweard*, which then decayed[30] a bit to *hlaford*, then *hlaverd*; by the thirteenth century it was *laverd*, then finally, about 1400, *lord*, where it stayed (lawdy be?). *Hláf* is what the word *loaf* looked like 1400 years ago, and *weard* is ward, or guard. The *hláfweard* was the controller, the guardian, of the bread and as such it referred to the male head of household; compare our 'breadwinner.' And one of the early words for servant or household member? *Hláfæta*, loaf eater.

Every lord should have his lady, and she, no less than her husband, came from a loaf of bread. She is *hláfdige*, *dige* being a form of the word that gives us dough, which as a verb meant to knead, to knead the loaf, knead the dough. About the same time and in the same dialect that *hláfweard* became *lord*, *hláfdige* became *lady*. It is no accident either that the word for bread or food does double duty as the word for money, though it is usually in the form of meat that it does that. Thus Latin *pecus*, cattle, gives us pecuniary, and in Old English its cognate is *feoh*,[31] which gives us *fee*.[32] I hardly need mention that both *bread* and *dough* still today are slang for money. Both lordship and ladyship are about the control of food at some primordial level at the primordial table.

The lord's loaf eaters are, in one sense, his companions; in another sense, they are his retainers, for he is their leader, their master. The loaf guard and his loaf eaters owe each other protection. By some aspirational norms, the retainers should avenge their lord if he is slain or die lest he be slain. But the risk of dying for their loaf giver is balanced against the danger lurking in the loaf eaters' appetites. (A household, no less than armies and smaller armed bands, marched on its stomach.) The loaf eaters can eat their lord out of house and home. They can eat him to death.

III.

From the Germanic world let us repair to biblical Israel, to the Book of Judges, before there were kings in Israel, after which we will return to dine at the Last Supper. Judges 19 tells the gruesome story of the Levite's concubine, perhaps the most appalling incident, among no small number of contestants, in the Bible. Here is a quick synopsis, and though it might not be readily apparent why this episode figures in a discussion of eating, feasts, food, and lords, you will see that it has much to do with the rules of hospitality and the obligations that guesting and hosting entail. It also has to do with obliging revenge.

A Levite from the hill country of Ephraim took a concubine from Bethlehem in Judah. She and her husband quarreled; she left him and went back to her father in Bethlehem.[33] The Levite went looking for her to patch things up, "to speak friendly unto her." Her father welcomes him and feasts him with food and drink for three days. The Levite sets out to return home on the morning of the fourth day, but his father-in-law prevails upon him to stay longer. Presumably three days was the limit a guest could stay before offering to leave, as in Iceland and Anglo-Saxon England. The text takes care to narrate the father's begging him to stay on day four and day five, accentuating the contrast between the hospitality that governed in Bethlehem in Judah and that of Gibeah in Benjamin, to which we and they are soon to be exposed. On day five they leave fairly late in the day, delayed by the father-in-law's insistence that they stay still longer. Evening comes, and they being close to the Jebusite city, Jebus, which the text says was what Jerusalem was called before it got a name change,[34] the Levite's servant suggests that they stay there. But the Levite mistrusts the hospitality of the Jebusites, a non-Israelite tribe, and so they continue on to Gibeah, a town in the Israelite tribal territory of Benjamin. There they find themselves after sunset in the central square with no place to lodge and no invitations forthcoming from the townsmen until an old man returning from his work in the fields takes them in. He is only a sojourner in Gibeah; he is native to the hill country of Ephraim, the Levite's own tribe and region. The text emphasizes that he is not a Benjamite. But Gibeah's natives are and they are also a nasty bunch, much like the ones who angered God enough to obliterate Sodom. They gather round the house and demand that the host put out his guest so that they can rape him. He resists: "do not do such an evil thing," he says:

> "Behold, here is my daughter a maiden, and his concubine; them I will bring out now, and humble ye them, and do with them what seemeth good unto you: but unto this man do not so vile a thing." But the men would not hearken to him: so the man [the Levite] took his concubine, and brought her forth unto them; and they knew her, and abused her all the night until the morning: and when the day began to spring, they let her go.[35]

The head of household offers the Levite's woman along with his own virgin daughter. Apparently, he is indeed lord over those to whom he has given hospitality. Nothing the Levite says or does denies that power to his host. But lest the host sacrifice his maiden daughter, the Levite, a gracious guest, relieves the host of his hostly burdens and takes upon himself the grim responsibility of what is going to be done to his woman. One wonders if by volunteering his virgin daughter the host 'earns' the right to offer his guest's woman, or is it rather that he is showing his good faith, that he is not taking a right he already has lightly? Or is it that by offering up his daughter he is hinting for the Levite to do just as the Levite does? In any event, it is not just the power a host has over his guest that is in evidence, but the obligation the host has to protect his guest.

The text treats the Levite's woman better than any of the men in the text treat her. It paints her end with pathos: "Then came the woman in the dawning of the day, and fell down at the door of the man's house where her lord (the Levite) was, till it was light . . . *her hands were upon the threshold* (a powerfully moving image)."

But what do we make of this?

> And her lord rose up in the morning, and opened the doors of the house, and went out to go his way: and, behold, the woman his

concubine was fallen down at the door of the house, and her hands were upon the threshold. And he said unto her, "Up, and let us be going." But none answered. Then the man took her up upon an ass, and the man rose up, and gat him unto his place. And when he was come into his house, he took a knife, and laid hold on his concubine, and divided her, together with her bones, into twelve pieces, and sent her into all the coasts of Israel.

Her body parts are sent to summon all Israel to take revenge on the tribe of Benjamin, which is well-nigh exterminated in the next chapter, only six hundred men surviving.

There is much of interest here—the story raises more questions than can be answered—but let us stick with food, to carving up meat, and ignore all the story has to say about hospitality and hostility, as well as gang rape, or the male guest being first choice of the rapists.

We are in the midst of a ritual here over which the Levite will officiate, but one does not quite know at what point to start the ritual action. When the Levite orders her to get up? He must see that she is dead. How else can we explain the coldness of the command in the face of what he knows is the truth, her hands gripping the threshold of the host's lodging as if beseeching succor/welcome/rescue? It is not that the Levite does not care for her. He would hardly have undertaken the burdensome trip to Bethlehem to retrieve her if he did not.[36] He refused to enter Jebus for fear that they would be at risk and not be welcome, hence his continuing on to Gibeah. Though we moderns recoil that he put her out, saving his own skin no less, she was going to be put out nonetheless by the host. He saves the host's virgin daughter, rather than his own wife.[37] This is, I would guess, less because the virgin is of higher status by being uncontaminated by male intrusions, though that may be some of it, than because she is of higher status by virtue of being the host's daughter, and I would guess barely twelve years old, if that.

The Levite is locked in by, of all things, the norms of gift exchange, repayment for hospitality. He hardly put his woman out blithely, as his subsequent actions show, for now he will, with stern will, set about avenging her, employing a ritual that will charge the nation to take revenge. This ritual requires the presence, the Real Presence we might say, of the victim. It is she who will summon the forces to avenge her.

Her body parts compel the nation to assemble. At that convocation of the people the Levite narrates his tale so that the horror is twice presented, once in chapter 19 as it occurs, and again in chapter 20 in his retelling it to the nation.[38] The people are outraged and enraged; they send messengers to Benjamin telling them to hand over the guilty Gibeahites, but Benjamin refuses, and now the whole tribe will justly pay for a crime not to be borne.[39]

Move forward about a thousand years to Jerusalem, to the Last Supper. Jesus celebrates Passover and is the head of the table, the guardian of the loaf, though the room that he and his disciples occupy is either rented or offered to him and his men for the occasion by a man whom Jesus counts as a reliable member of his following. Since this is Passover, the bread is unleavened and not something we think of today as a loaf. Nonetheless, it is divisible into twelve pieces, and he will break the bread and pass the cup. But Jesus adds a gloss to the traditional bread breaking, itself already symbolic of sacrificial dismemberment, by drawing out the symbolism and personalizing it: "And he took bread, and gave thanks, and brake it, and gave unto them, saying, 'This is my body which is given for you: this do in remembrance of me.' Likewise the cup after supper, saying, 'This cup is the new testament in my blood, which is shed for you'" (Luke 22.19–20).

He is asking his loaf eaters, his household men, to eat him, to consume him, by consuming his food. But this he says is not merely his food, but his very self, the bread and the wine IS his flesh and blood in the way it was when the *hláfæta* (loaf eater, retainer) ate his *hláfweard's* (lord's) loaf, his lord's sustenance and substance. Europe nearly exterminated itself over how metaphorically this eating of one's lord should be understood, the Roman church taking it literally and officially after 1215, seeing rather perspicaciously what it means to eat someone's food in a world of serious scarcity.[40] In this view, the bread is the host, in *host's* double sense of the head of the table who gives hospitality and the sense of victim, the paschal lamb of the Passover sacrifice.[41] But whether it is one or the other, both clearly are eaten; that is what loaf eaters do to their lord.

Feeding gods, as when we sacrifice animals to them, butchering them on the altar, and then eating the sacrificial victim, and eating the gods themselves seem to take place at the exact same moment. Animals used to feed the gods are often one form of the god. Thus, bulls were sacrificed to Zeus and eaten by the sacrificers, and lambs (and bulls) to Yahweh, whether in the form of the Lamb of God or the lamb as the substitute for Isaac (and also eaten by the sacrificers); it is much as Odin did when he says he sacrificed "myself to myself."[42] Not only are we what we eat, but it seems that we also worship what we eat, and make our main food into gods. Those who eat fish worship fish gods, those who keep sheep worship lambs and rams, or their god takes the form of their chief food source as one of his avatars.[43]

Look at it from Jesus's disciples' point of view: they are asked to eat their master and they are also eating *with* him. They are thus companions in its root sense—those who eat bread together—but they are also in the unequal relation of those who feed *on* their lord, who is their loaf of bread, and who also breaks his body apart for them to be sustained.

I would not have brought up the Levite's concubine if I did not think that Jesus was making an *explicit* reference to that horrific scene in Judges, though as far as I know, none of the figural interpretations that Christians imposed on the Hebrew Bible to prefigure the New Covenant saw the Last Supper prefigured in the dismemberment of that woman's corpse. But Jesus did. He knew covenants needed flesh and blood, body parts, to bind, and so would a New Covenant, a New Testament. And he knew his Hebrew Bible, that soon-to-be Old Covenant, quoting passages frequently by heart. Jesus is ripping himself into twelfths (the number of disciples intentionally matching the number of tribes) and hands the pieces to those men who would travel to the limits of his kingdom and beyond, to what? To bind them to avenge the death to be done him by those wicked men asking for his body outside the door of *his guest lodging*: "Now men, tomorrow I will be abused and die from it. This bread and blood binds you to avenge me, just as the Levite's woman's broken carved up body obliged the nation to avenge her." He is consciously employing the proper ritual to charge others to avenge him. Strange, is it not, that his *first* words after parting his body and blood are to announce that one of them will betray him, thus avenging himself on Judas, but said in a way that only Judas can fully understand what has just been said (Luke 22.21)?

This revenge-charging ritual that uses the victim's body and blood to oblige others to take revenge for the victim appears across numerous cultures. Some of the most famous scenes in the Icelandic sagas enact the ritual.[44] But it is everywhere; barely attenuated forms of it are performed by Abel's blood, which calls out to God; it is performed 'virtually' by Hamlet's ghost charging his son to "remember [him]" as in "this do in remembrance of me"; and Saul, in Gibeah!, hacks into twelve pieces his yoke of oxen to muster Israel to attack Jabesh Gilead (1 Sam. 11.7), and not least in Judges 19. It is manifestly the ritual form Jesus imbues the Eucharist with.[45]

There are other startling analogies between the Last Supper and Judges 19. I already mentioned that Jesus is celebrating the Passover in another man's home who is generously giving these newly arrived men a place to stay. They are lodgers just as the Levite and his concubine are. Judas, who is one of the twelve, plays the role of Benjamin, one of twelve that is to be done in, for betraying the nation. Unlike the Levite who bypasses what he assumes will be the hostile city of the Jebusites, Jebus/Jerusalem, Jesus enters that city to rest there and finds it as hostile as the Levite assumed it would be, even though Jerusalem is now, as an official matter, if not a spiritual one, Judean.[46] Moreover, my disciples, there are bad men outside the door, just as there were in Gibeah, which is but a stone's throw from where we are seated today. Jesus even advises arming themselves, to buy swords (Luke 22.36). Those Benjamites outside the door, the sons of Belial, do they not prefigure the Jews of the Gospels, the ones waiting to grab him and violate him once he finishes his Passover meal? You might well want to resist, but all I am trying to do is make sense of this well-attested vengeance-obliging, obligation-creating ritual, widely dispersed across cultures, and Jesus's clear enactment of it at this particular moment. That IS there. He surely knows he is performing the same ritual that the Levite performed: the Levite when his people violated rules of hospitality as to him, and Jesus when his people violated the rules of welcome as to him.

There is also a possible pun lurking beneath the text. The Hebrew word for bread is *lechem, or lehem*. It is the 'House of Bread,' Beth*lehem*, where the Levite's concubine is from, and where Jesus was born; they share a place of nativity. They also share having their bodies divided into twelve parts, one really, one figuratively. Jesus is speaking Aramaic, though Luke is rendering it in Greek, but in Aramaic the word for bread, *lachma*, clearly cognate with *lechem,* can commonly mean flesh or meat, as it does in its modern Arabic reflex. The pun on bread as meat is not there in Luke's Greek, *artos,* but in one place in Leviticus (3.11) Hebrew *lechem* also, as in Arabic and Aramaic, clearly indicates flesh, meat. So when Jesus says this *lechem, lachma* is my body, he is not being all that metaphorical: bread and flesh can be the same word, the Word made flesh, in a sense.

Calling for revenge? Is that what Jesus is really doing? Let me make a more modulated reformulation of exactly what I am arguing. I am not saying Jesus is telling his disciples to go out and kill, to take blood revenge, though my ancestors can attest that his later followers might have come to understand their mission in those terms, but that was later. The ritual obliges them in no uncertain terms to carry on his mission by binding them with this most powerful of obligation-creating rituals, binding them to 'remember' him, not by having him in their heads in a mental act of remembering, but by proving their memory in action, in something like the sense the ghost charges Hamlet to remember him.[47] This bloody-token ritual can be put to various uses: to charge the nation to go to war to avenge the Levite's concubine, to muster it against Nahash as when Saul employs it, or to go out and take over the world with good news.

In the end revisit the common explanation of the necessity of the Incarnation and Crucifixion I touched on earlier (p. 29): that since man is not at the level of God he cannot ever make adequate recompense for his first disobedience, so God sends himself in the form of his only begotten son, a human, to be killed and sent back to him as adequate amends for man's original sin. Only the death of God in one of his personae can work as an equivalent to get even for the wrong done God in another of his personae. That is something of a revenge story, is it not?

As a strange irony that played out over the longue durée, look who actually ends up biting the dust in this drama—not the Son, who is made or is confirmed as Lord by his resurrection. The Son, Jesus, the God of the Christians, ends up supplanting the Father, the God of the Jews, over the course of a couple of centuries. We could even compare mythologies to make the claim not as far-fetched as it might first appear. Cronos castrates his father Uranus, Zeus by some accounts does the same to his father Cronos, and that is in effect what the Son ends up doing to God the Father. The Father is not killed by the Son, but he does not sire any more sons does he? The Father ends up emasculated by old age and by his only Son and heir. Jesus Christ ends up turning Yahweh, that warrior God, that storm god, into a white-bearded old man. Imagine Yahweh's chagrin seeing that he had been displaced by a baby in a manger for part of the year or by a young man of low rank for the rest of it. The New Testament, the young covenant, transformed the Hebrew Bible into the Old Testament, and Yahweh grew old along with it, ending in it as the Ancient of Days in the late—that is, the young—Book of Daniel. Christianity wanted its God young. In fact, it would not let him get old, having him die in the prime of life, for absolutely no one would think it much of a sacrifice if Jesus died at my age, an old man of seventy-four.

PS: A short version of this chapter was presented to the Christian Law Students Association at the University of Michigan in 2017 (and again in 2019), some of whom I feared might be offended and be moved to stone me, but they, except for one who walked out (maybe just to go to the bathroom, though she never came back), asked good questions. That talk took something of the form of a medieval disputation, for it was followed with a counterpoint and rebuttal given by my evangelical colleague and friend, Professor Dan Crane, who, in accurate imitation of those medieval disputations between Jews and Christians in which Jews were well advised to plead faintly or die, had an audience who would declare him the victor no matter what (he had orchestrated the event). But he, a son of missionaries, knows how to seduce with the Word; even I was moved by the attractive face he gave to his Lord as he prepared to die, before I, within a few decorous seconds, reverted to the views presented here.

8

Odds and the End

THE WORD *odd* ALREADY received some philological attention in "The Messenger" (chapter 5), where the 'oddman' made a brief appearance. 'Oddman,' you may recall, was one way Old Norse named an arbitrator. There, *odd* was contrasted with *even*, a way of classifying numbers. The oddman was the necessary third person needed to settle a dispute between two contending parties, to bring them back to some hypothetical evenness.

In the expression 'odds and ends' there is not the least suggestion of numerical unevenness. What is indicated is a pile of stuff that does not fit, or is left over, remnants that no one knows what to do with except perhaps to use them for kindling, if wood or paper; or, if bits of cloth, to serve as a bonanza for a rag-picker of old; or, for a modest offering of a mix of food qualifying as leftovers, to offer a friend who stops by. The 'odds' and 'ends' of 'odds and ends' are not meant to contrast with each other, as would *odd* with *even* or *end* with *beginning*, but they are meant as synonyms; 'odds and ends' is, to invoke the fancy rhetorical term, a pleonasm. The OED suggests that 'odds and ends' is "probably an alteration of *odd ends*, found in same sense much earlier" than the first recorded appearance of 'odds and ends' in 1740.[1]

If, as the OED suggests, the phrase 'odds and ends' is an eighteenth-century expansion of the sixteenth-century *odd ends*, might it be that the 'and' worked its way into the middle of the phrase 'odd ends' by the luck of *and* so nearly reproducing the phonemes of both *odd* and *end*, off-rhyming with both, as *odd* and *end* do with each other? They are all near homophones exerting a kind of homophonic attraction on each other (homophones are intent on plaguing me [see pp. 3–4]).[2] Moreover, the main job of *and* is to be a go-between and bring things together, much as the 'oddman' does, so that two parties can cease to be 'at odds.'[3] Then add 's' to *odd* for balance, and more euphony, and it seems that the earlier 'odd ends' was ineluctably fated to metamorphose into 'odds and ends'; that *and* could just not keep itself from squeezing in between 'odd ends.' Words and phrases can make your head spin when you start to think about them. They might qualify as one of the true wonders of the world.

Two earlier chapters directly (chapters 1 and 2) and another obliquely (chapter 3) made much of odds in a different sense: as in "the odds are against you"—hence the discussions on luck, and the less than even odds of good things happening, at least by those stricken with that cursed self-referentiality I called the narcissism of negativity. To remind you, it is that intrusive sense that makes us feel that the gods have specially singled us out to dump disappointments on us and, crucially, that we play an oversized causal role in bringing down these disappointments not just on ourselves, but on the universe, simply by hoping or wishing for a certain outcome. Either we did not undertake the proper rituals to propitiate the Powers That Be or, no less likely, we *did* undertake the rituals and performed them flawlessly. But the gods refused to accept our offerings, accepting rather our opponents', not because of their merit, but solely to thwart our desires. Never mind that as many people on the other side are subject to the same irrationalities, for such are the workings of the narcissism of negativity that I (we) firmly believe that the Powers That Be do not focus on others with the same will to torment as they direct toward me (us). That is how narcissism works. My torments are worse than theirs for the sole reason that they are mine, even if I know that that is not a morally defensible position. I should be ashamed to assert it. But I doubt that they are any more moral with regard to their torments. Our mutual overvaluing of ourselves at the expense of others is in equipoise.

Let's put *odds* as probability and *odd* as thirdness aside and get to a small scrapheap of odds and ends with three stories whose main claim to oddity is that I think them a good way to draw the book to its end if you will excuse the epilogue that follows this chapter, and you will find that they resonate in various ways with what has gone before.

Story 1: *A Fight to the Death*

This story was told to me by a colleague, Nina Mendelson, when I thought to talk to her about curses and maledictions, especially of one particularly witty saga example.[4] Her tale recalls themes in the chapters on luck and the conservation of good things. The risk of being cursed was an *éminence grise* in those discussions, especially in the most seemingly benign of encounters. The deep belief, or rather the niggling fear, is that good fortune is the very manufactory of misfortune. The story also revisits the magic of words by vividly illustrating a standard matter in the philosophy of language associated with the Oxford philosopher J. L. Austin and what he called 'performatives.' These are words or phrases, like 'I do' in a wedding ceremony or pleading guilty in a criminal case, that *do* something, rather than merely state or tell something. Austin set forth what he called 'felicity conditions' that must be met for performative utterances to have effect, as, for example, that they were not said in a theatrical performance or in a quotation or in indirect discourse.[5] But in certain circumstances the words might be so powerful, so magical, that the felicity conditions are always met, that is, that the mere saying of the words brings about the change whether you meant it to or not, that they are brutally never a joking matter. Saying them in quotes or in a theater performance would not undo their transformative power.

The dramatis personae are two six-year-old girls in a Wisconsin farming community near Madison, nearly fifty years ago, one a farmer's daughter (FD), the other a daughter of grad students (GD), wanting to live closer to nature but still within driving distance of the university. The girls are standing in line for their first gym class on their first day of first grade and strike up a conversation:

FD: You know, my grandma is sick, and if she says 'Jesus, I want to die,' she will die.
GD: I don't believe that's true.
FD: Then say it.

GD: I'm not going to. But you just said it.

FD: That doesn't count because I didn't mean it.

No shortage of IQ in this high-stakes encounter, and such enmity arising within seconds of meeting each other too. It is not even clear who won the battle to the death, for that is what it is, or if that is an exaggeration it is a very small one, for they think death's shadow is shading the encounter. The cold lethality of FD's "then say it" is worthy of heroic literature. What did GD do to prompt that lethal response? Did FD think that GD was calling her a liar? Was it a look on GD's face? Was it because she doubted Jesus's power to kill (or to save, depending on how you look at it)? Was FD standing up more for grandma's power to "call him from the vasty deep"? But GD is not fool enough to rush in and invoke Jesus in this way to prove FD wrong. GD is a Jew, and even at age six a Jewish kid is wary enough about Jesus to suspect that if she, a Jew, were to say "Jesus, I want to die," he might be only too willing to grant the request, or else his worshiper might take it as a warrant to act as her Lord's agent and spare him the task.

But how do we characterize FD's "then say it"? The imperative in this case is before anything else a dare, a challenge to GD's courage. Obviously not only boys issued or felt the stakes of these dare challenges, and those who think otherwise because such toxicity is wholly the stuff of puerile masculinity should read a saga or two, or have grown up in my family, or have gone to my grade, middle, or high school. It is hard for a self-respecting kid to back down from a dare, though FD's imperative is ambiguous enough to be taken as an order that begs for refusal because it assumes in FD the right to give GD an order. GD's refusal can be read variously as a refusal to play, a refusal to obey, a refusal to accept a challenge, or a refusal to back down. GD is not in the least bit craven. She hits back with a powerful defense. These girls are very evenly matched. You think, implies GD, that you won because I don't have the guts to say it? I do not have to prove those words won't kill me, because you just showed they didn't kill you. (And with a hint of prudence: why should I test your Jesus a second time?)

These two girls deployed one of Austin's important contributions to linguistic pragmatics with so much more wit and economy than it is discussed in most academic literature. FD, without invoking the highfalutin notion of 'felicity conditions,' nonetheless mobilizes that very concept to reserve to herself the final say. She argues, quite astutely, that she did not say the magic words in *propria persona*, but ventriloquized what her grandmother 'could say' if she wished to but had not in fact said. "Jesus, I want to die" thus got *not said* twice, for neither she nor her grandmother had properly said it. Those words were doubly hypothetical, not one set of scare quotes were mobilized but two. And her proof that she did not meet the appropriate felicity conditions is that she is still very much alive, and so is grandma.

This battle to the death with death averted by ventriloquization is too close to call to declare victory for FD, for she is playing with a more generously tempered deity than were she playing with YHWH whose name, unlike Jesus's, was not allowed quotation marks. The mere saying of the tetragrammaton, the name of the LORD[6] (YHWH), was, in the view of some, lethal no matter what, as even writing it with the proper vowel points in Hebrew might kill and thus was studiously avoided.[7] Everywhere it appeared it had to be fully euphemized. According to rabbinic accounts, only the high priest could say it once a year, so that for about two thousand years or more no one really knew how it was pronounced. Some biblical philologists, not fearing getting wasted by divine fire, declared that 'Yahweh' is pretty close to what was said, which might help explain why those who pronounce it 'Jehovah' are still fearlessly ringing your doorbells. Jehovah is almost certainly not how the tetragrammaton was pronounced, for Jehovah's sequence and quality of vowels were openly borrowed from the vocalization of YHWH's standard euphemism Adonai, the common word for lord or master.

In grade school I too felt the dangers of various divine names. I "would get such a kind of gain giving . . . here about my heart" at certain moments singing those beautiful Christmas carols, providing much-needed relief from the unbearable Rudolf and Santa Claus either kissing mommy or coming right down Santa Claus lane, to say nothing of the God-awful Hanukah songs we were cursed with. I loved those carols so much I feared I was surely giving offense both to their God and to Yahweh whose wrath I was risking by traitorously belting out, "oh come let us adore him, Chri-ist, the Lord." Was singing this in music class or "for real" in the Christmas program itself sufficient to put scare quotes around the lyrics, or around me? That all-inclusive 'us' in "come let us" in effect rendered me a craven convert. But "God Rest Ye Merry Gentlemen" set my adrenaline to rushing; it gave me chills. A Christian could surely sing it with greater comfort than I could, but not with greater joy. The song simply transported me.[8] And I felt like I was going to have to pay for that transport.

Incredible that my colleague, Nina, remembers this incident from her first day of real school: first grade. This was not kindergarten child's play to her mind, and as I have hinted, it has something of the quality of an heroic tale, Achilles going against Hector, Beowulf against Grendel or Grendel's mother. So, then, who started it? GD by suggesting FD was a liar? Or FD by raising this rather strange subject as a conversation opener before they even knew each other?[9] One could say, "oh kids, you know they say funny things; they voice whatever transient thoughts pass through their minds." More astute is Elizabeth Bowen with this chilling observation:

> With no banal reassuring grown-ups present, with grown-up inter-vention taken away, there is no limit to the terror strange children feel of each other, a terror life obscures but never ceases to justify. There is no end to the violations committed by children on children, quietly talking alone.[10]

Didn't FD have to know what she was up to by making lethality her choice of topic for her first conversation with this other girl, her soon-to-be classmate for the year and a few more thereafter? What placed these two girls one behind the other on such an important day in the life course of a child?

> What brought the kindred spider to that height,
> Then steered the white moth thither in the night?
> What but design of darkness to appall?—
> If design govern in a thing so small.[11]

Story 2: *What's the Point? Or Spikes of Despair*

That grand existential question and accompanying answer, "What's the point? There's just no point at all," plagues postpuberty well into one's twenties—I would say "your" twenties were I more confident about the generalizability of my own experience, which I am frequently accused of generalizing too readily as if I were Everyman. With more than occasional, yet manageable, revisitations during the decades from twenty-five to sixty-five, that Q and A, however, returns in full adolescent force when you are deemed "fit" to be set adrift on the ice-floe of retirement, if you can manage to find an ice-floe these days—it won't take long to melt if you do. This 'what's the pointism' is not not giving a damn, which is too defiant, too focused in its hostility, and too heroicized by Clark Gable–esque overtones. Nor is it not caring not to give or not give a damn, that sentiment expressed by the shoulder shrug of indifference. 'What's the pointism' is more despairing, more dead-ended, though it could just as likely lead to the eat-drink-and-be-merryism of Ecclesiastes, no less than to the unrelenting bleakness of *Lear*, of which more soon.

My youngest of four children, Hank, short for Harald in the Norse spelling, which I insisted on once my wife firmly nixed my half-hearted suggestion that we name him after my favorite character in world literature, Skarpheðinn of *Njáls saga*. With one kid named Odin in one of his siblings' classes at school, I thought it might be worth a try, taking my turn at the obnoxious whimsy that has characterized naming patterns in the last forty years or so. Where have all the Bills and Dicks gone? To Wills and Richards, everyone. And forget about Chuck, for reasons similar to those that took down Dick.

Hank was the most cheerful of kids, always happily entertaining himself, living in an active fantasy world, never bored as he acted out various imaginary characters in different voices in the next room or out in the yard. He was never embarrassed enough to stop when we walked through and tried not to burst out laughing. One night, when he was nine, a week before his eldest sister, Bess, eight years older, whom Hank was very close to, was heading off to college, I found him in bed sobbing. I asked him if he were okay. He continued sobbing and shook his head. I said, "Are you sad Bess is leaving?" "No." "Well, what is it?" Says he, with a catch in his voice amidst the sobs, "There's no point; there's just no point at all to anything."

I was rather taken aback at these words from someone his age, but I said, "Well, Hank, I can't tell you that you're wrong in the grand scheme of things" (some will argue this was not exactly the wisest concession to make, but I fully understood the sentiment and hardly wanted to tell him he was wrong, which would not lessen his misery without a longer discussion). I continued: "But most people do not entertain that worrisome thought until they're older" (a bit of flattery to help cheer him up and to register my own quiet satisfaction at the precocity of his misery, half attributable to my genes, the levels of shameless vanity hitting new lows with the cult of DNA), "and you will find it keeps reoccurring and then mostly goes away" (I was as yet unaware, that being some sixteen years ago, that it would return with a vengeance once I hit my late sixties). "But, Hank, there was this French guy more than 250 years ago who said the point is to cultivate our garden. What he meant was the best way to keep those big miserable questions about the purpose of life at bay and not think too much about the grand pointlessness of everything is to keep your thoughts and actions and goals confined to things you can learn how to do and take some small control of, to the extent that that is ever possible, and achieve some modest, but genuine, satisfaction in things learned, and in tasks well done." He understandably kept sobbing. I wondered why I had not immediately, as was my wont, passed off such duties of consoling, advising, and emotionally supporting the kids to my wife. I headed straight downstairs to ask her what was up with him. Her response? "Oh, he just read a book on the environment."

I do not believe that he was worried that he would be part of the mass extinction that was foretold and well underway, but that somehow the continuity of the world largely as he knew it was at the core of what he thought the whole point of his life was. We naked mole rats (I beg pardon of the innocent real naked mole rats) made in God's image have done a real job on his fifth and sixth day of creation.

'What's the pointism' has an uneasy relation with our narcissism of negativity. One is a sign of giving up, the other of caring immensely. One has us taking to bed and turning our face to the wall; the other has us calculating, strategizing, worrying, running to and fro, trying to intercept the malevolence or the practical jokes the gods are planning to send our way, to dash some hope, or put a dent in our new car. The narcissism of negativity has us doing nothing as grand as turning and facing the wall, but rather knocking on wood, or making sure we get a benign seat number on a flight, or not hanging up after what seems like years of being put on hold, for we know the second we hang up is the second they would have gotten back to us. Finally, perhaps in a moment of rational indifference, we shrug our shoulders and get on with it.

There is a powerful Middle English lyric that is perhaps the most pointedly condensed gloomy statement of 'what's the pointism' possible, matching the unfathomable nihilism of *King Lear*. I will render it in the original and then in a translation that will keep as much of the original as possible, which is not much of a challenge as you will see. Know that the letter þ, called thorn, is an old rune that renders the sound of the digraph 'th' as in 'thorn.'[12]

> Erþe toc of erþe, erþe wyþ woh,
> Erþe oþer erþe to þe erþe droh,
> Erþe leyde erþe in erþene þroh—
> Þo heuede erþe of erþe erþe ynoh.[13]

> Earth took of earth, earth with woe,
> Earth other earth to the earth drew,
> Earth laid earth in an earthen trough [coffin],
> Then earth had of earth, earth enough.

Match that for bleakness, the incantatory force of the repeated words and sounds: poetry at its best, the sheer brutal economy of it. Humanity appears only as dirt; I would say this vivifies the tired idiom of "dust to dust" if we allow that there is any vivification present in this verse at all. All is death. Life is nothing but death in a false and easily-seen-through disguise that gives it a very brief capacity to be consumed by woeful self-loathing before it drops back into inert insentience. Earth draws other earth to itself to procreate? To kill? To grow? But only after 'birth' had taken place with woe in the first line. In any event, it all leads to burial of dirt in the dirt by dirt. As dead as earth is, it has, however, for a brief moment, an inner life capable only of impatient disgust, sick unto death with itself: *Þo heuede erþe of erþe erþe ynoh*. That extraordinary last line, with earth repeated three times, expresses just how totally fed up life is with its pointless self, as earth stomps itself back into the ground where it belongs.

An ancient commonplace makes much of the fact that the first thing a baby does when born is cry, unless it is stillborn. Lear puts it this way: "When we are born, we cry that we are come to this great stage of fools" (4.6.200). I recall but cannot find, even with the aid the computer provides, a genre of Middle English lyric I read in graduate school that has us born with cries of AAAA and dying with tears and groans of OOOO, the Alpha and Omega of human life, weeping and wailing at beginning and end, and in between, a vale of tears, valleys of the Shadow of Death, a Dark Forest, whether of Dante's grand imagining or as the Dark Wood menaced by industrialization intruding upon the fading bucolic world of the less grand, but undoubtedly wonderful, Ratty and Mole.

These common laments of the miserable lot of most humanity suggest that if there is a point, it is that suffering is the point. Christianity is not the only tradition that puts suffering at its core, but it is the only one I know that made it its logo: Christ on the cross, its signature emblem, is before anything else an image of pain and cruel death, perhaps not unfairly understood as an exercise in pedagogy meant to teach God what it means to be human. It then becomes also an emblem of love, in which God gives up a beloved son. It is assumed that this God knows what it means to love a son; otherwise, how could he have come up with the cruel idea to torment Abraham with the command to sacrifice Isaac? We need some assurance, for it seems that God, when contemplating sons, at least firstborns, thinks first of smiting them or demanding that they be sacrificed to him, not only the first-born Egyptians but the first-born Hebrew too, who must be ransomed from God's claim to kill him (Exodus 13.15). This offer to redeem the newborn for a price is a benefit that he gives his people. From the Son's viewpoint, the Christian account, it is the son's love, more than the father's love that is revealed, for he undertakes his end as a gift to mankind, making their suffering his, so that humankind has something sufficient to placate the father. That is but the tip of the iceberg for the connection of love to suffering. Every teenager dumped by his or her first love is something of an expert, as is every parent of a soldier killed in battle.

Dead-endedness, cries of pointlessness, laments of life's meaninglessness, life at best as a cruel joke, filled with pain and suffering, produce some of the greatest and most powerful writing. With that exquisite quatrain, *Erþe toc of erþe*, compare the grandeur that is *King Lear* or the Book of Job.

Return to the scene in *Lear* in which the Duke of Cornwall captures the material essence of the human eye as vile jelly and thus provided me with the title of a chapter by doing so. Vile jelly is one kind of ocular metaphor; the eye as window to the soul is another: one to be seen through, the other to be looked at in horror, dangling down a cheek, or stuck on a knifepoint. Gloucester, now blinded, issues a bitter lament that reformulates a sobbed-out cry of "what's the point" by finding a point of sorts, a negative point, one of motiveless cruelty and sadism, a point paradoxically pointless, for its very pointless malignity is meant only to provide entertainment for bored deities: "as flies to wanton boys are we to th' gods, / they kill us for their sport"(4.1.41–42). The metaphor lowers gods to prepubescent 'innocent' boys, as it lowers the rest of us to flies; everything is relocated downward. Yet as flies Gloucester can finally find these metaphorical human insects worthy of pity, while the metaphorical gods become real schoolboys, human young, the real sources of evil who school the gods in how to do it up right.

Don't we believe, without having to go all the way with Dostoyevsky, that suffering, surely in some settings, is efficacious and therefore in some sense meaningful? You want to get into shape; it better hurt, for no pain, no gain. Why is it that I prefer any antiseptic I put on a cut or scrape to sting? If it is one of those salves that do not hurt, then goodbye placebo effect. Admittedly, to call that suffering is a bad joke, for it is perfectly within your power as to how much or how long you endure it. In our largely pain-is-optional culture the odds against the virtue of suffering in silence have gotten longer.

Arthur Koestler's soon-to-be-executed Rubashov distinguishes between senseless suffering and suffering that makes sense, the former caused by unjust human social arrangements, the latter a necessary feature of embodiment, or "biological fatality"; it is this latter that we have managed to make largely optional, the former we seem to have a will to re-create for disfavored others as soon as we begin to congratulate ourselves that we have evolved into kinder, gentler creatures, an utterly risible claim that sold quite well fairly recently to a slew of wishful thinkers.[14] But Rubashov's distinction would not capture the virtue in Christian suffering, which gives sense to both of Rubashov's types of suffering, for both require patience and both provide the grounds for the theological virtue of hope. This kind of making a virtue of necessity puts us back into our zero-sum world again.

Yet as contemptible as our lives of instant gratification are, the nonstrenuous pursuit of pleasure, it is still not clear that we are morally any worse or better than the residents of some impoverished third-world village in which suffering and scarcity abound. The most brutal stories of selfishness are stories of what happens during serious want. Siege warfare provides the horrific commonplace setting in which humans are reduced to cannibalism and carrion eating, the food in either case being the flesh of your 'loved' ones, whom you either kill to eat or are happy to see die so they can be eaten. The model description of such horror is the curse in Deuteronomy 28.52–57. Too much suffering is not very good for virtue, and I suppose no suffering or the elimination of its prospect is not good for it either. But we still have an accurate sense that virtue in conditions of suffering or of dire scarcity demands a whole lot more virtue of a virtuous person than virtue exercised in conditions of plenty. The widow's mite is greater in moral units of value than the rich person's endowment of a hospital. We thus rise one small step above the utter nihilism of "Erþe toc of erþe" where nothing matters at all, not even the widow's mite.

Suppose you believe that suffering ennobles somehow. Can it survive Gloucester's flies' winglessness? Can there be any meaning in the suffering of those flies,[15] any less than in the suffering of a Jew in a death camp or in a cattle car, besmeared with vomit, urine, and feces on the way there, or lined up naked with her child before the ravine at Babi Yar, calling on her God, but having to use a euphemism, because his name YHWH was lethal too? Or perhaps cursing him, or did he no longer matter, because in her terror she was wholly occupied by wanting to make sure to hug and warm her shivering and frightened child, if the little girl had not been forcibly separated from her and already been thrown into the pit? Or, as in the curse in Deuteronomy, could she hardly care about her child or anyone but herself under such conditions? It is a story of degradation all the way down; the suffering of the victims degrades all but a rare few of them, but their degradation pales beside that of the foulness of the souls of the victimizers. It all totals out to less than zero sum, to as low as you can go, down to

0° Kelvin on the moral scale, where you join the scum who deny it ever took place.

Good thing for Hank I stopped with Voltaire's anti-big-gloom-and-doom, anti-grand-posturing in the defiant shake-your-fist-at-God style, and felt that parental wisdom meant not expanding or expounding upon the kid's Job-like cry to show him how rich the tradition he had hit upon is.[16] And my mere dipping my big toe into the grim darkness of that tradition for the last few pages should perhaps be understood as a kind of knocking on wood to placate the gods for the presumption implicit in the very modest optimism of the Voltairean position, that there will be a garden to cultivate and there will be harvests to be gathered in, at least "until the dragon comes."[17]

Story 3: *Mr. Boffin Redivivus*

Lighten up, Miller, lighten up. Look on the bright side. Never mind that as you write the Anglo-American world is committing suicide; that you have acid reflux, aching joints, and a left big toe pulsing in limp-generating pain; and that you, like the nine-year-old Hank, are consumed with 'what's the pointism' about writing yet another book. After my last book was published in January 2017 with a title I dare you to pronounce—*Hrafnkel or the Ambiguities*—it having been finished a year earlier for it takes that long to see it through the refereeing and publishing regimen, I was empty, and decided to retire to half time, and then fully to retire, this year. I could not justify going on were I not to write and I had nothing left to write about. What was I to do to kill or fill time? I took to reading: rereading books I had read long ago that I loved or ones I had never finished that I should have loved or should have finished even if I did not love them, and finally those I had lied about and said I had read or even admitted I hadn't read but now would do penance and read them. A subcategory of such books consisted of very long multivolume works that I had only read parts of here and there. So I started by reading all six volumes of Gibbon's *Decline and Fall* and all of Plutarch's *Parallel Lives*. I then took a small respite and decided to re-read one of my three favorite Dickens novels—*Our Mutual Friend*—to find company with a relatively minor character, a feckless young solicitor, Eugene Wrayburn, who captured my fancy as an undergrad.

Now enter my daughter, Bess, a struggling actress, the very same whose imminent departure for college years before was what I had mistakenly thought was the cause of her little brother's tears. She too loved *Our Mutual Friend* and when I told her I had been filling up the vacuum of my end of days with reading Gibbon and Plutarch, and that I was now just about to begin rereading *Our Mutual Friend*, she said, "Dad, you've become old Boffin." She was referring to the suddenly rich Boffin of that novel who was illiterate and hired the peg-legged rogue Silas Wegg to read to him so he could gain some rudiments of culture and thus render himself more worthy of the new social position his sudden riches had raised him to. What did Wegg read to old Boffin? Gibbon and Plutarch. Bess perfectly saw her father had become a combination of Boffin and Wegg, fool and knave.

So? Go, bid the soldiers shoot.

9

Epilogue: Go Litel Boke amidst a Flurry of Auto-Antonyms

I BID GOODBYE TO you the reader with this commencement speech given on December 22, 2017, in which I bade goodbye to the fifth of the University of Michigan law school class that were known as summer starters and thus graduated a semester earlier than the majority of their classmates who began law school, more conventionally, in the fall of their first year and graduated in May of their third year. The summer starters have to suffer in-house 'talent' for their commencement speaker, while the May graduates are treated to more prominent outside speakers, though I must confess that when those speakers are announced I sometimes have to Google to find out who they are. Like the host/guest and hospitable hostility of chapter 7, the address treats of words that can mean themselves and their opposites. Now commence the commencement address:

You had me for Property, and what you learned, if you learned anything, is that I sometimes take frolics and detours. These often dealt with the histories of words: remember how we started out noting that *property* is the same word as *propriety*, and that *to owe* and *to own* come from the same Old English root? Those words yoked contraries, binding rights ever so tightly with duties.

My graduation talk will also be a detour; instead of talking about milestones or even millstones of debt incurred reaching this particular milestone, I'll talk about the words *graduation* and *degree*. (You could

145

hardly expect me to give a go-nobly-forth-and-conquer commencement speech, could you?)

When you got to law school, you thought the word *sanction* meant
to have permission, to be allowed to do something. You soon learned
that *sanction* was also the general word for the punishment meted out
for doing something unpermitted or disallowed. *Sanction*, it turned
out, could mean itself and its opposite. Linguists call such words auto-
antonyms,[1] and they are not all that rare, like *cleave*, to stick to, and
cleave, to split, as in the cognomen of my favorite earl of Orkney,
Thorfinn the Skull-cleaver. Remember the important concept of *seisin*?
It produced both Modern English 'to seise' (with an 's' meaning to put
someone into possession of land) and 'to seize' with a 'z,' to take it away
from him. Some auto-antonyms arise by a different mechanism, when,
say, reciprocal actions, like give and take, collapse and point the same
way: thus, a *caregiver* and a *caretaker* are identical. Or, when someone
decides to beat you to a pulp, he can equally be said to be *taking* it to
you or *giving* it to you. And, wouldn't you know, *graduation* and *degree*
also qualify as auto-antonyms, especially *degree*. Here's how.

Graduate comes from the Latin *gradus*, meaning 'step.' And the same
word gives us *grade,* as in the grades I gave you, to the pleasure of very
few of you. So *graduation*, the word, is linked with grading both in
practical terms, as you know only too well, and in etymological terms,
about which I am presently informing you. No, not entomological,
not the study of bugs, but etymological, the study of word origins.
But don't diss bugs, for they, not you, shall inherit the earth, probably
in your own lifetime.[2] And this short digression on bugs also involves
Latin *gradus,* for the *gress* in *digression* is the participial form of the verb
derived from *gradus*. Digress is to step away or, as is my wont, to step
astray.

That's all obvious; how could the *grad* in *graduation* not be related to
grades, both as words and as a cruel fact? This graduation today means
you get a degree, but not so obvious is that the word *degree* also comes
from *gradus*. Prefix *gradus* with *de* and of course you get *degrade*, as in
humiliated, but yes, you also get *degree*, for that *gree* is merely what
early French did to Latin *gradus*. Losing that 'd' in *gradus* is but part of
the process that gradually turned Latin into French. *Degree* and *degrade*
are the same word, just said with a different accent. (Notice too that

poor D, the letter grade, has also disappeared from your transcripts unless you are truly special, for in the last twenty years that D has been inflated and thus morphed into a B– or, in some of my colleagues' seminars, into an A.)

When *degree* came into English, it simply meant 'step,' even referring to stairs in a house well into the nineteenth century,[3] and stairs can lead down as well as up, but *degree*'s twin, *degrade*, kept to the dark side in the social world, only pointing downward, as in being chucked down the stairs, or just falling down them, a constant anxiety at my age, and utter humiliation in either case.[4] But even *degrade* can point upward and march with the saints, as when food packaging, like humans who are but food for worms, unless mummified or cryonified, is made bio*degradable*.

A line from an old blues song comes to mind: that "old TB" or in another version "that woman" is "killing me, killing me by degrees." But not only can you be killed by degrees but also that killing can be graded too, as in the first or second degree; now there is a *graduation* for you, a scaling of wrongs, and *scale* too means step or stairs. So murder and murderers get their degrees, no less than you law students do. Compare too how in another auto-antonym-like instance the 'third degree' can be the least offensive (as when grading crimes) or the most serious (as when grading burns).

Grading can be horizontal too. Road graders make sure everything is leveled. *Grading* of this sort squishes ups and downs into a plain old plane, all gradations and degradations, and thus degrees, eliminated. *Grade*, the word, auto-antonyms itself to death in dizzying fashion.

By the way: for those of you with a master's as well as a BA or BS degree, your law degree will be your third degree. For you, this degree suggests figurative torture, the third degree, though you are surely the better for having survived it.

Some of you may have read Nabokov's *Pale Fire*; if you haven't, make sure to do so before you die. That book, in large part, plays on *gradus*, and on *gradus*'s French form *gree*, for it is a homophone with the color (or noncolor) *gray*, which is but one of the shades of pale in *Pale Fire*. The murderer in this strange mystery is Jakob Gradus; he goes by various aliases—Jack Degree, or Jacques de Gray—and the novel follows him step by step as he closes in on his victim and kills him in the first degree.

Nabokov and the French pronunciation of *degree* give me warrant for a concluding digression on *gray*. Gray shades to black or fades to white, colorlessness in both directions, whited out or blacked out. (Is it properly spelled 'ey' or 'ay'? There is a story to tell there too, but I will spare you.) Remember my digression a couple of years ago, on the word *black* sharing an Indo-European root with French *blanche* (white), English *blank*, or with a long vowel variant yielding modern English *bleak, bleach*; the word *black* thus got whited out by meaning itself and its opposite.

But why should I end so bleakly, blackly, or blankly, all the same word you now see? Instead, let me say I have a special bond with you; you were my last Property class ever. And though good luck is a very scarce resource, the proprieties of this occasion demand that we all pretend that there is an infinite supply of it so that I can wish ALL of you the best of luck for the law degree you've earned, even if the word *law*, a word that English stole from Old Norse, and like the word *degree*, doesn't point upward either, because it means to lay *down*. When your parents said that they were laying down the law, they were being redundant.

Let me conclude with a blessing: May all your future interests[5] be reasonably bright and may they vest, if at all, just in the nick of time. And what in the world is a 'nick' of time? Therein lies a faux auto-antonym, for Old Nick, the devil, might just be St. Nick, Santa Claus upside down and in disguise, who on this gray day, the second shortest of the year, stuffed your stockings with law degrees penned in ink, coal black.

NOTES

~⟢◆⟣~

Introduction

1. My non-American friends were blessedly unacquainted with "better than the alternative," hence my explanation. To be noted is that the "wit" of the phrase supposedly lies in its observing the taboo on directly naming Death by employing a euphemism as is often the case for naming the very sacred, the very dangerous, and the very profane.
2. The same motorcycle made a brief embarrassed appearance in *Losing It*, 231.
3. Snorri Sturluson, *Edda*, chs. 46–47.
4. See Ker's classic *Epic and Romance* published in 1897.
5. Peter O'Toole at something like six foot two or three inches was thus miscast as Lawrence, but the two, facially, bore an uncanny resemblance.

Chapter 1

1. I deal with some of the same issues rather differently in a discussion of Hamlet's defying augury in *Losing It*, ch. 16, and how Audun's luck works in *Audun and the Polar Bear*, 71–77.
2. New Zealand provided the complement to Canada in an earlier draft and then an Australian white supremacist showed up on the Ides of March 2019.
3. Germany soon went the way of New Zealand, getting back to its own kind of normal with an October 2019 Yom Kippur bombing attempt on a Halle synagogue.
4. Montaigne, *Essays*, II.12 (p. 584).

5. See McDonough, 15.
6. Wolff, 89.
7. Bao Ninh, 31. We might also hazard the suggestion that such anxieties about luck are a near-human universal; what will vary across cultures are the types of rituals employed to ward off evil, the kind of demons that must be outfoxed, the various things that count as good or bad omens, and the different ways of divining, whether by bird flight, sheep livers, chicken guts, coin flips, astronomical events, the weather, and so forth.
8. Mark VII (Max Plowman), 54.
9. It was that debacle in Seattle in January 2015 that prompted the first briefer iteration of this chapter in the *Chronicle of Higher Education*.
10. Lat. *spes*, n.f., *spero*, v.
11. Austen, *Sense and Sensibility*, ch. 4 (p. 17).
12. For Machiavelli's views on how to treat Lady Fortuna, see chapter 4, n.15.
13. Gluckman, 23.
14. I made this up as a parody, and then I found that the field had just come up with something very closely resembling it as a serious theory; see Wrangham.
15. A fancy way of saying the punishment should fit the crime in some emblematic way, thereby making the justice poetic.

Chapter 2

1. Thus Montaigne, *Essays,* I.14: "everyone knows that death, called the dreadest of all dreadful things, is by others called the only haven from life's torments, our natural sovereign good, the only guarantor of our freedom, the common and ready cure of all our ills; some await it trembling and afraid: others bear it more easily than life."
2. See Aquinas, Supp. Q99 A1.
3. See Vlastos's discussion of various pre-Socratic medical and cosmological theories in which the organizing principle is of getting even, of balancing out—that is, of justice.
4. Not that some will not try. See n. 13 in this chapter on measuring happiness.
5. This from Montaigne, which he takes from Tacitus's *Annals* 15.67–68:

    One may reprove the greatness of soul of those two soldiers who answered Nero back to his face: one of them, when asked by Nero why he wished him ill, retorted: "I loved you while you deserved it; but since you have become a parricide, a fire-raiser, a mountebank and a chariot-driver, I hate you as you deserve"; the other, asked why he wanted to kill him, replied, "Because I can find no other remedy to your continual misdoings." *Essays*, I.3 (p. 12).

6. Nietzsche reproduces a text attributed to Tertullian on the delights of watching the damned suffer in hell; see *Genealogy of Morals* 1.15. Aquinas,

Supp. Q99 A1, reply to objection 4. See the discussion of the possibility of fear in heaven in my *Mystery of Courage,* 202–4.

7. The doctrine has its scriptural warrant in the Annunciation, Luke 1.28.

8. See OED s.v. dosis n. and Pokorny s.v. dó, 223–24.

9. See my *"Why Is Your Axe Bloody?,"* 75ff.

10. See further p. 128.

11. If the number 'one' gives us 'atonement,' see further p. 74 and accompanying footnotes for how the next odd number 'three' gives us the means to get back to even.

12. If the pie gets bigger, it is no longer a closed system subject to conservation, but let us continue with the strength of our beliefs notwithstanding.

13. The work is associated with Ronald Inglehart of the Political Science Department at the University of Michigan.

14. Lewis, ch. 5.

15. For a much grimmer view of laughter than I cursorily present here, see Hobbes, *Leviathan*, I.6: "those Grimaces called LAUGHTER"; and a more extended treatment in his *Elements of Law*, I.9.13: "There is a passion which hath no name, but the sign of it is that distortion of the countenance we call LAUGHTER, . . . men laugh at the infirmities of others, by comparison of which their own abilities are set off and illustrated."

16. On the social and psychological mechanisms of getting our emotions to the proper level, see Adam Smith, Part I.

17. I have seen the tale told in so many different places that I cannot for the life of me find to which ethnos belongs the credit for first telling it. But it describes any academic department, no less than a peasant village. The subject is nowhere more cleverly treated than in Swift's "Verses on the Death of Dr. Swift."

18. Quoted in Blok, 33.

19. Leave it to the genius of the sagas to joke about these issues. A certain Sturla takes to bed overcome with depression at the death of his inveterate enemy, a woman who tried to stab out his eye years earlier but managed to badly cut his face nonetheless. When asked why he was not delighted with her death, he wittily noted that with her passing all the delight he took in tormenting her sons died with her, and thus a good portion of the purpose of his life; *Sturlu saga,* ch. 36, and see my "Threat," 20–27, for a full discussion.

20. I do an extensive reading of *The Merchant of Venice* in my *Eye for an Eye,* ch. 6.

21. I couldn't refrain from extensive ridicule of the field of positive emotions in *Losing It.* I am lumping happiness and joy together here, but one could distinguish them. I want to avoid any mention of *jouissance*, which (to the extent I can understand anything in Lacan) involves conservation, the observation being that sexual pleasure and pain are often hard to

distinguish. Even if orgiastic pleasure might outweigh the frustration and tension leading up to it, if we add in the *tristesse* after it we might well start to approach zero.

22. Elster, 64n4.

23. The utilitarian exercise of tallying costs and benefits of an activity can still make sense in our system of pessimistic folk beliefs if it counsels avoiding policies that sum out to *less* than zero.

24. See my *Anatomy of Disgust*, 170–78, for a more fully argued account, and also for an argument of equal and mutual contempt as the basis of democratic equality in ch. 9 of that book. Elias's view of the Middle Ages, by the way, offends medievalists by turning smart, cagey, and often surprisingly decorous medieval people into children. Note too that back in the time of Judges 3 (see pp. 85–86), Eglon's servants respect his privacy when they believe he is relieving himself and thus do not enter upon him.

25. The view from the contemporary chronicles that *Y. pestis* was not a respecter of persons, with rich and poor, young and old, all felled at roughly the same rates has been subject to revision by biological anthropologists working with plague burial sites. The unhealthy and malnourished went at higher rates; see, for example, the fascinating work of Sharon DeWitte.

Chapter 3

1. This chapter is a revision of a talk I gave at a conference on competition in beautiful Konstanz, Germany, on April 19, 2017. It deals with some themes raised in the previous chapter from a different angle. My take is rather unlike views of competition one would get from economists or game theorists. My account is more psychologized.

2. See Payer, chs. 1–2, for various medieval theological positions on desire, sex, and bodily functions in Paradise.

3. Consider the argument Pope Urban II is said to have made in his call for the First Crusade (1095): "Let none of your possessions detain you, no solicitude for your family affairs, since this land which you inhabit, shut in on all sides by the seas and surrounded by the mountain peaks, is too narrow for your large population; nor does it abound in wealth; and it furnishes scarcely food enough for its cultivators. Hence it is that you murder one another, that you wage war, and that frequently you perish by mutual wounds. Let therefore hatred depart from among you, let your quarrels end, let wars cease, and let all dissensions and controversies slumber. Enter upon the road to the Holy Sepulchre; wrest that land from the wicked race, and subject it to yourselves. That land which as the Scripture says 'floweth with milk and honey.'" From the account of Robert the Monk, full text here: https://sourcebooks.fordham.edu/source/urban2-5vers.asp#robert.

4. On Japanese honor in the context of other honor systems, see the excellent essay by Edwards.
5. *Eyrbyggja saga*, ch. 37.
6. *Guðmundar saga dýra,* ch. 16. See also *Bandamanna saga*, ch. 10, where the game takes the form of a person choosing people he thinks to be his equals. Not unlike the Icelanders, we play similar ranking games; they are an internet staple.
7. Seating arrangements are often subject to aggressively enforced laws governing behavior at kings' and princes' courts. See, for example, Sven Aggesen's *Lex Castrensis* in which the default punishment for a retainer violating court rules was to be seated one seat farther down (§5 and pp. 35, 37): "no man could be moved from his usual seat without shame and dishonor"; see also Saxo Grammaticus (10.18.5) for what we might call a 'seat court' to adjudicate disputes over seating. Saxo, as did Sven, attributes these rules to Cnut the Great. See further p. 114.
8. See Martin McDonagh's *Seven Psychopaths* (2012), where Christopher Walken's Quaker enacts a version of the role I am supposing here.
9. Browne, *Religio Medici*, §55.
10. Franklin, *Autobiography*, Part II, 652–54.
11. The competition within monasteries is often noted.
12. These moments of temptation to abandon the rigors of the ascetic enterprise are much the subject of the *Life of St. Anthony* (d. 356), one of the most popular and influential of saints' lives, the reading of which triggered St. Augustine's conversion (*Confessions*, 8.14–19); for an online English translation of the Greek text see https://www.patristics.co/on-the-life-of-st-anthony/.

Chapter 4

1. I did, however, accept an invitation to participate in a conference on disgust at the Université de Liège in 2013. The people organizing the conference were serious scholars, the papers good. A version of this chapter appears in the conference's proceedings as "Epilogue: Do I Disgust You? (Or Rather, You Me?) mes frères, mes sœurs, mes semblables?"
2. I have since had one more short revisit; see Miller, "Dégoût."
3. *Chronicle of Regino of Prüm*, sub anno 870, in MacLean, 163; see also ibid, 193. The Icelanders were not given much to blinding. In one famous incident it is not clear that they gouged deeply enough to cause much harm; see *Íslendinga saga*, ch. 115, and discussions by Lawing, 159ff, and Gade's tour de force. Also see ch. 2, n. 19 and ch. 5, n. 18.
4. For example, Curtis et al.
5. There are accents we loathe, but this is less about the quality of sound itself than a judgment about the people who speak with that accent. They need not be low-class accents, many of which are more appealing

euphonically than more educated accents. The mid-Atlantic accent of, say, Katherine Hepburn elicits sociological fury from a midwestern American such as I. Auricular disgust is not the issue at all; pretense is. Regarding the sounds of bodily functions like vomiting, see the mercifully brief discussion in *The Anatomy of Disgust*, 82–83.

6. I am taking the adult's-eye view here. In *Anatomy of Disgust*, 13, I discuss the problem of paring back the acute disgust mechanism you struggle to instill in your toddlers to toilet train them only to find they are now so horrified by feces that they are afraid to wipe themselves, or to accept that a carrot is not revoltingly contaminated if it touches some mashed potatoes on their plate.

7. Voltaire, s.v. Nudité.

8. Though there is some overlap between disgust and contempt, the two can be fairly distinguished for a significant part of their respective domains; see more fully my *Anatomy of Disgust*, 31–33, 206–34.

9. In this light consider Freud's description of a kiss: "contact between the mucous membranes of the lips . . . in spite of the fact that the parts of the body involved do not belong to the sexual apparatus but constitute the entrance to the digestive tract"; is he joking? *Three Essays*, I.2.

10. Thanks to my daughter Bess Miller for alerting me to this. It is all about deuterostomes (which include us) as against protostomes (e.g., nematodes), but see the modification of such opposition in Martín-Durán et al.

11. Thus the success of the website People of Walmart: http://www.peopleofwalmart.com/, which can be seen as something of a parodic homage to lower-class style.

12. Gerald of Wales, *Gemma Ecclesiastica*, 2.17: *hispidus, macilentus, scaber, et horridus*.

13. The Old Norse verb is *flekka*, cognate obviously with English *fleck*.

14. To Luigi Guicciardini, December 9, 1509, in Atkinson and Sices, 190–91, which I have slightly modified in ways too insignificant to note.

15. I feel reasonably confident one should not be too generous to Machiavelli's unconscious considering his treatment of Lady Fortuna in *The Prince*, ch. 25, where beating and rape work better than softer persuasions: "it is better to be rash than timid, for Fortuna is a woman, and the man who wants to hold her down must beat and bully her. Like a woman, too, she is always a friend of the young, because they are less timid, more brutal, and take charge of her more recklessly." Can you imagine what your luck would be like if you raped Lady Luck or Fortuna?

Chapter 5

1. Social theorist Georg Simmel invests the move from two to three parties with the most significant of transformational powers in the evolution of social and political complexity (118–62).

2.   Simmel notes that impartiality can be achieved in two main ways, via the independence of the third party or via his equal attachment to both sides.

3.   Old Norse *oddi*, also see ch. 8, n. 3 and my *Eye for an Eye*, 11–16.

4.   OED s.v. umpire, n. The 'n' shifted, as is not uncommon in English, with 'an uncle' becoming Lear's Fool's 'nuncle'; compare 'another,' as when we say 'a whole nother matter.'

5.   Andrew Cecchinato, a postdoc in legal history at the University of St. Andrews, supplies this in an email when I told him of the 'oddman,' the Hebrew word for 'arbitrate,' and the origins of 'umpire.' He writes: "there is in antiquity a preference for odd numbers. Virgil offers an eloquent attestation of such belief in *Eclogue* VIII.75: *numero deus impare gaudet*, "god delights in an uneven number." This leads to 'thirdness' or, in Italian, *terzietà*. This is the condition of the virtuous judge. It is more than simple impartiality, it is full independence."

6.   Though an intercessor is surely a go-between, he usually plays quite a different role than a classical mediator. He is usually understood to act on behalf of an inferior. See pp. 90–91.

7.   Simmel starts with a positive view of the rationalizing effect of impartial mediation, which makes the disputants focus on hard issues, neutralizing the effects of the passions, but later admits that any story of the dispassionate third party is incomplete without a discussion of *tertius gaudens*, the advantage (and joy) gained by the third party from the misfortunes of the principals (154–62). This is another point to add to the discussion of Schadenfreude in chapter 2.

8.   Goffman, *Presentation of Self*, 149. Nowhere are the moral difficulties facing the go-between, as well as the possible moral culpability of the parties using him, more movingly dealt with than in L. P. Hartley's masterful novel, *The Go-Between*.

9.   Groebner, 43–44.

10.   Pepys, VI.44.

11.   *Njáls saga,* ch. 44; see discussion in my *"Why Is Your Axe Bloody?,"* 102–3.

12.   I am much indebted to my daughter Eva Miller, an Assyriologist, who put me on to the ancient Near Eastern materials. I also acknowledge a large debt to Samuel A. Meier's fine book *The Messenger in the Ancient Semitic World*.

13.   Compare this to Greek *epistle*, meaning that which is sent, and *apostle*, meaning the messenger.

14.   For a fuller account, see Meier, 11–12.

15.   *Amarna Letters,* sigilled conventionally EA.

16.   A kingdom stretching roughly from modern eastern Turkey to northern Iraq. They spoke Hurrian, a non-Semitic, non-Indo-European language. Neither it nor its cognate languages survive.

17.   These letters are part of a negotiation of a marriage alliance; Tushratta is also disappointed in the amount of gold sent with the message.

18. Consider this letter from Šulgi (A), king of Sumer (c. 2000 BCE), answering a complaint from his messenger Aradĝu (B) about his mistreatment at the hands of one of Šulgi's vassals, Apillaša (C), to whom he was to deliver a message from Šulgi (A). Aradĝu (B) is repeatedly humiliated, kept waiting at the gate, then coerced to receive a meal that they spill on him, while he insists that all hospitality must first await the delivery of his message. Apillaša (C) seems to take offense at Aradĝu's (B's) insistence that he state his message before being entertained. Most remarkable is King Šulgi's (A's) response to Aradĝu (B) in which he tells him to stop complaining, that he, Aradĝu (B), well knows that Šulgi (A) must let Apillaša (C) have some room to play the role of a 'big man' on his own turf: "If I do not make Apillaša (C) feel just as important as I am, if he does not sit on a throne . . . if his feet do not rest on a golden footstool, . . . **if he does not kill or blind anyone, if he does not elevate his favorite over others—how else can he secure the provinces?**" (emphasis supplied); see *Letter from Šulgi to Aradĝu about Apillaša,* http://etcsl.orinst.ox.ac.uk/cgi-bin/etcsl.cgi?text=t.3.1.02#. Oh the perks and joys of lordship.

19. *Ljósvetninga saga,* ch. 7; *Hrafnkels saga,* ch. 20; and see discussion in my *Hrafnkel or the Ambiguities,* 69–70, 199.

20. See Althoff, 158.

21. See the complaints of the messenger in n. 18 in this chapter.

22. "The Report of Wenamun," in Lichtheim, 226.

23. Gregory of Tours, 7.14.

24. *Hittite Diplomatic Texts,* No. 2, §45, p. 18.

25. According to Meier, in the ancient Near East "diplomatic immunity was at best a messenger's dream" (76–77). No grace, obviously, was allowed the enemy's couriers and messengers seeking aid from their allies or communicating with segments of their own forces. Athenians captured Spartan envoys on their way to the Persian king and killed them without trial, a trial Thucydides seems to suggest they were entitled to, for defenses might have been available to them (2.67). In Spain, Caesar had the hands of intercepted messengers cut off before sending them on their way; *The Spanish War* §12, also §18 in *Caesar,* 329, 402.

26. This incident makes for one of the stupider scenes, among many, in the appallingly bad movie *300* (2006).

27. Herodotus, 7.133–36. Medieval annals and chronicles show numerous violations of messenger immunity. In 1183, Henry II's sons, the Young King and Geoffrey, either wounded or killed their father's envoys to whom they had specifically granted truces; *Gesta Regis Henrici,* 1.298, cited in Strickland, *War and Chivalry,* 52.

28. See, for example, *Royal Frankish Annals,* anno 782.

29. Joab brilliantly rubs David's face in this shameful killing of Uriah by purposefully provoking his anger over the unnecessary loss of men who

got too close to the wall and then quickly having the messenger assuage his rage by revealing the identity of one of those 'unnecessary' losses.

30. The fear that the messenger had delivering bad news could be matched by an omen reader doing the same, interpreters of dreams and omens being messengers of sorts. A certain Óspakr in *Njáls saga* (ch. 156) asks to be held harmless before delivering his unfavorable interpretation of certain omens to one Bróðir, and when granted a pledge of peace, Óspakr still waits until night to deliver his views, "because Bróðir never killed at night."

31. Montecuccoli, 156.

32. Within two and surely within three centuries had the Rab'shakeh spoken in Aramaic, the common soldiers on the wall would have understood him, but c. 700 BCE, when Sennacharib was invading, Hebrew was still the people's language.

33. Perhaps Hezekiah's officials could have bribed the Rab'shakeh to deliver his message in Aramaic. Septimius Severus, for example, bribes envoys sent by the senate declaring him a public enemy to deliver a message more to his liking that he could let his troops hear; *Historia Augusta: Severus*, 5.5–6 (193 CE).

34. Aristotle, *Rhetoric*, 1379b.

35. *The Prayers of Paheri*, in Lichtheim, 19.

36. See Michalowski, 3.

37. This matter is discussed more fully in chapter 6, p. 98.

38. Gregory, 8.44 (*legatus*); also 7.20, but here Fredegund is operating more in the Icelandic style of sending a servant to join the household of the target.

39. Suetonius, *Augustus*, c. 49.

40. "The Teaching of Vizier Ptahhotep," in Parkinson, 253.

41. *Hittite Diplomatic Texts*: No. 2, §59, p. 20; see also EA 32: "in this matter I do not trust Kalbaya. He has indeed spoke it as a word, but it was not confirmed on the tablet."

42. Montaigne, *Essays*, III.1 (p. 896). The ancient Near Eastern messengers, as well as those in Gregory and elsewhere, appear often to ventriloquize their messages, relaying them, but assuming the person of the sender as he delivered the message. This means that the messenger in his role as his master's voice could be the object of displays of deference as if he were the master himself, not merely a whipping boy for his master as has been more in evidence in our examples up till now. See the discussion by Meier, 152–53.

43. There are other risks that the sender bears. If his message is spurned or his messenger insulted, mocked, or killed, the sender will most probably lose face; at the very least an act of enmity has occurred.

44. See my *Audun and the Polar Bear*.

45. Gregory finally resorts to *argumentum ad hominem*: Arius, he says, died of uncontrollable diarrhea, his entrails expelled through his anus, a point

Gregory makes each of the five times Arius is mentioned in his history (2.23 [two times], 3 prol, 5.43, 9.15).

46. For a nice example of such nested interceding, see Koziol, 76.

47. But it can work the other way, as the vulgar marriage broker has a privilege to gain access to fathers higher in status than he is, if they have marriageable sons and daughters.

48. *Eyrbyggja saga,* ch. 9; *Guðmundar saga dýra,* ch. 3 (where it is stated that he will join against those who do not listen to him).

Chapter 6

1. There is a view that only in the last few centuries was something Charles Taylor (130–31) called "radical reflexivity"—the awareness of one's awareness, the experience of experiencing—a possible psychological experience. I am dubious about theories that would accord to the average iPhone user a more complex mental life than the average medieval cleric or blood-feuder, though I hardly think their mental lives would be the same. See my "Deep Inner Lives."

2. A reflex of the word *authentic* was not likely to be used in this setting, though it could have been used to describe legal documents, or even a person as the proper holder of an office or position in the early fifteenth century. See MED s.v. autentik.

3. See Shklar, ch. 2, 45–86.

4. The adjective enters English in the fourteenth century, the noun not until the eighteenth. See OED s.vv. authenticity and authentic. The noun does not take on the meaning that I suspect the conference organizers meant it to have until the twentieth century.

5. JSB (Jewish Study Bible) punts on the translation:

   Moses said to God, ". . . what shall I say to them?" And God said to Moses, "Ehyeh-Asher-Ehyeh." He continued, "Thus shall you say to the Israelites, 'Ehyeh sent me to you.'" (Ex. 3.13–14)

   In a footnote to v. 14, JSB (p. 111) says it is "probably best translated as 'I Will Be What I Will Be,' meaning 'My nature will become evident from My actions.'" That does not quite mean that his actions will not at times be arbitrary, but it confirms that his name is meant to be something of an unanswerable riddle.

6. See Southern, 50.

7. Stendhal, 2.8, p. 298.

8. "Inside the Whale," 1.509–10.

9. I am not engaging the volumes of philosophical writing about the self, sense of self, identity, or personhood. Let me only say that my own anxieties about fraudulence and of failed authenticity are in no way improved or worsened whether the self is there or not. If the self,

whatever it is, is really there, it could still be doubted as Hume and others have, and if it is fictional or a mere convenience, linguistic or psychological, it could nonetheless be believed in as most of us do.

10. Herodotus, for example, 5.63, 6.75.

11. For developing the theater metaphor with a host of insights, see Goffman, *Presentation of Self*, though he mostly avoids the issue of the 'self.' I do not sign on to the "it's all discourse" position. I imagine Samuel Johnson refuting Foucault, not by kicking a stone as he did when claiming to refute Bishop Berkeley, but by kicking Foucault in the shin.

12. By saying that, I do not mean to elevate victimhood into the only authentic status, politicized as that has become. It is as susceptible to pretense as any other role. Moreover, in most of my experiences of wanting to disappear in shame I fully deserved the miserable state I was in.

13. Freud, *Jokes*, 8.81.

14. Not only that, but the idea of Freud bowdlerizing the joke was not mine; it was a reading I borrowed and duly credited to Cuddihy's *The Ordeal of Civility*, 24. Cuddihy's falling victim to the Strachey translation did very little to undercut the consistently insightful observations he makes throughout his treatment of the difficulty that Jews, especially Ostjuden, had/have in understanding or becoming adept at the manners and forms of civility that characterized the higher levels of European society.

15. Both Christianity (obviously) and Islam (in a more attenuated sense) are daughter religions (schisms?) of Judaism. Neither could have arisen were there not Jewish scripture.

16. See http://gutenberg.spiegel.de/buch/der-witz-und-seine-beziehung-zum-unbewussten-933/1.

17. For scriptural warrant of the Son as coeternal with the Father, see Hebrews 1.2, where working through the Son, God made the world, and so too John 1.1ff. See Milton's rendition of the role of the Son in the wars in heaven: "Son of my bosom, Son who are alone / My world. My wisdom and effectual might" (*Paradise Lost* 3.169–70).

18. It is not as if genuine insight into the complex relation of the anti-Semite's own core self to the Jew cannot be had by a confessed anti-Semite, as well as a very keen sense of what Jewishness might be. A must-read: Gregor von Rezzori's *Memoirs of an Anti-Semite*. There is a brutal joke Jews tell each other mocking their own self-hatred: "What is the definition of an anti-Semite?" A: "Someone who hates Jews more than is absolutely necessary."

19. Rozin and Fallon, 32.

20. Recall chapter 4, p. 66, where the naked beautiful bodies of Germans on the beach were rendered invisible by the naked ugly ones, ugliness overpowering beauty in its battle for my attention and control of my imagination.

21. See the discussion in Shapiro, ch. 1.

22. As per Goffman's brilliant paranoid essay "Normal Appearances" in his *Relations in Public*, ch. 6.

23. "Sham converts for material reasons?!" How about to avoid being butchered, or having one's children taken away? https://en.wikisource.org/wikzii/Catholic_Encyclopedia_(1913)/Tom%C3%A1s_de_Torquemada'. See also Mel Brooks's musical comedy version of Torquemada: https://genius.com/Mel-brooks-the-spanish-inquisition-lyrics.

24. For the revelation of how I got the Ian in my name, without an ounce of self-hatred on the part of my parents or grandparents, though not without some on my part when I write it out as a nom de plume even though it is my real name, see *Faking It*, 132.

Chapter 7

1. Though the talk in Missouri was out there for the viewing, I nonetheless revised it to make it more appropriate to medievalists and in that revised form I presented it at Oxford for the Annual Medieval Studies Lecture (2014), and then recycled it yet once more with moderate revisions in St. Andrews for the Annual Lecture of the Institute of Legal and Constitutional Research (2017), hoping that no attendees had been at any of the other occasions nor had surfed the web and discovered I was also wearing the same jacket and tie.

2. *Egils saga*, chs. 44, 71–72.

3. On fear's power to displace anger, see Adam Smith, VI.iii.9–10.

4. See *The Anglo-Saxon Chronicle*, E version, entry for 1012.

5. Sven Aggesen's twelfth-century *Lex Castrensis*, §5, p. 35, also chapter 3, n. 7; see also the boy made the daily target of thrown bones at mealtime in *Hrólfs saga kraka*, chs. 33–34.

6. It might still be true that whom you eat with is more important than whom you sleep with; in any event, both eating with and sleeping with are fraught activities that couple pleasure and disgust, necessary bodily functions, with rich social and cultural mediation. Just as there are those you must eat with, there are also those with whom you are not to eat with under any circumstances: excommunicants, for instance. See *Þorgils saga skarða*, ch. 56, where the bishop says that the farmers may give the excommunicated Thorgils food rather than suffer him robbing them when he shows up paying them a 'visit,' but then they must feed any leftovers to the dogs. Thorgils's status pollutes the food.

7. *Hávamál*, sts 42, 45. See the clever rendition, "The Cowboy *Hávamál*," by Jackson Crawford: https://jacksoncrawford.com/the-cowboy-havamal/. Mauss starts his classic book on gift exchange with an epigraph quoting *Hávamál*. On the poison in the gift, see pp. 28–29.

8. See *Pactus Legis Salicae*, II.1, c. 46, pp. 286–89 (Drew trans, 110–11). *Beowulf*, vv. 2194, 2404, shows an analogous lap-laying transfer, in one

case of a sword and in the other of a jeweled cup. There is a Norse reminiscence in *knékast* (3.39), a knee or lap toss, which is part of a ritual of property transfer confirming a betrothal; see von Amira §65.8, p. 645. King Guntram adopts his nephew Childebert II with a ritual that looks like the stick ceremony (Gregory of Tours, 7.33). There Guntram used a *hasta* (a spear), not a *festuca*.

9. NGL I.208–9, *Frostathings-Lov*, IX.1. In Iceland, two *sáld*s of flour (*mjölsald*) were sufficient for the St. Olaf's day drinkfest in the early twelfth century; *Þorgils saga ok Hafliða*, ch. 10.

10. Nothing brings home the anxiety prompted by the scarcity of calories more vividly than that the Icelanders agreed to accept Christianity only on condition that they still be allowed to expose their newborns (1000 CE). But by the twelfth century the laws required all infants to be raised up no matter how deformed (*Grágás* Ia 3). We might consider infanticide as a kind of postpartum abortion, given how difficult it would be to accomplish the same prepartum.

11. On the modern useless child becoming the priceless child, see Zeliser; the term 'useless child' is hers.

12. Grønbech more than a century ago rightly noted that food and drink legalize the wedding as much as bedding (ch. 6, p. 281). It should be noted too that exposed babies were often wrapped up with some food in their mouths. I take that to be a way of assuaging what had to be misgivings, even guilt, at such dirty work by supposing that by so providing they were not actually killing the infant and could construct a compensatory fantasy that the infant would be found and raised up, by wolves if not by humans.

13. Both the OED and MED miss 'flesh' meaning specifically penis. See, for instance, Coverdale's translation of Gen. 17.11–14: "Thus shall my couenaunt be in youre flesh for an euerlastinge couenaunt. And yf there shal be any manchilde vncircumcided in the foreskinne of his flesh, his Soule shalbe voted out from his people, because he hath broken my couenaunt." https://www.studylight.org/bible/mcb.html.

14. Herodotus also reports that the "Arabians" use the blood of the contracting parties to seal an agreement (3.8), and not surprisingly the Scythians (4.70); see also Tacitus, *Annals* (12.47) for securing an alliance with blood squeezed from the tips of the bound thumbs of the contracting parties.

15. See Faraone.

16. NGL I.33, *Gulathings-Lov*, ch. 62; ch. 61 waives the ale requirement if freedom is granted by the king or if the slave paid for his own freedom or acquired his freedom by prescription, for which he had to live as if a free man for twenty years or more.

17. NGL I.33, *Gulathings-Lov*, ch. 63.

18. Cf. the Roman funeral feast on the ninth day, named the 'ninthday,' *novendialis*.

19. NGL I.14, *Gulathings-Lov*, ch. 23.
20. NGL I.51, *Gulathings-Lov*, ch. 115. Regarding the debt court and transfer of title, see Grønbech's remarks about the necessity of drinking to seal a deal in his own time (late nineteenth to early twentieth century): "Without a cup to soften the parting with the pig just sold, and confirm the joy at the shining dollars paid, it is hardly possible, among the peasantry, to buy or sell at all, and if a man have a weak stomach or a weak head to look after, he must excuse himself by an assurance of his sincerity: 'The bargain stands, for all that'" (281).
21. *Hlophere and Eadric*, c. 15 (Liebermann I.11, Attenborough, 20–21). This same imposition of liability for a host appears in a collection of laws from some five centuries later known as the *Leges Edwardi Confessoris* §23. The text is in Latin except it switches to English when it states this same rule: "quod Angli dicunt, tuo niht gest, þridde niht, o[g]ene hine": "as the English say 'two nights a guest, third night your own household member'" (O'Brien, 182).
22. Thus the law that provides that no one is required to maintain more than two third cousins who are the illegitimate children of the same man unless he is castrated; *Grágás* Ib 26.
23. Pokorny, 1.453. For words meaning themselves and their opposite, see chapter 9, and recall *fastidium*, p. 58.
24. This is a fortuitous homophone, 'host' as victim comes from a different root than the one producing host/guest; see Pokorny, 1.452–53. The communion host is from Old French *oiste, hoiste* from Latin *hostia* victim, sacrifice.
25. See Bosworth-Toller, s.v. þreát, II. http://www.bosworthtoller.com/, and my article "Threat." See also n. 6 in this chapter regarding a band of excommunicants showing up.
26. See *Egils saga*, ch. 81, on the visit of Einar Helgason to Egil. One was generally required to board up to five people on the way to weddings, spring Things, and so forth, but it is assumed that the stay would only be for the night; *Grágás* Ia 27, II 31.
27. *Laxdæla saga*, ch. 47: such was the shame for people to have to do their 'business' inside that those so humiliated said it would have been better had a few of them been killed instead. But no one says it would have been better had *I* been killed rather than suffer such shame. The ones so lamenting are offering up virtual bodies of some other household members, not themselves. But we are thus given a nice account of how scoring would work in the shame game being played.
28. Compare the inheritance rights that accrue to a host in the Norwegian *Gulathings-Lov*, ch. 113, NGL I.54, where it has a special name—*gesterfð*, lit. 'guest inheritance.' If a man hosts another who dies there, then if his heirs do not appear within three years, the host takes what the dead man had with him so long as its value does not exceed three marks. Iceland

had an analogous rule, but without the particularized terminology of
gesterfð (*Grágás* Ia 228–29).

29.   Thus Green, 194.

30.   I do not mean to be making any moral or even linguistic judgment by
using the word *decay*. I am merely using it to describe in this case the
loss of phonemes and the shortening of the graphemic representation of
the word.

31.   By Grimm's Law Indo-European *p* became *f* in the Germanic languages;
compare Latin *pater* with *father*, Latin *pisces* with *fish*. Latin *pecus* and Old
English *feoh* are thus the same word.

32.   *Cattle* and *chattle* are the same word entering English from different
French dialects, though, obviously, not cognate with *pecus* or *fee*. On yet
another linking of bread and money, see Kilger, 274ff: "in the antique
conceptual world and even on into that of the Middle Ages, coins stood
in a metaphorical relationship with the harvest and so with food. . . .
The nominal value of the coins was related to a specific quantity of grain,
which guaranteed its metal contents and weight."

33.   Concubine here does not carry any pejorative sense. The Hebrew text
calls the Levite her husband, and her father is referred to by the proper
Hebrew term for father-in-law and he as his son-in-law. It is also not the
case as in the Authorized Version (AV) that she "played the whore against
him." Though the Hebrew does employ the root ZNH to describe her
actions, literally to prostitute, the text and subsequent translations such as
RSV and JSB rightly understand the 'whoring' as metaphorical, referring
to her leaving him, to her quarreling with him; it is the act of leaving that
is the 'whoring.' The Levite is clearly on good terms with her father, who
also has no problem receiving his fleeing daughter, which he might well
have refused to do had she played the whore.

34.   That Jerusalem was earlier Jebus is not right as an historical matter; see
JSB 19.10n. But the reference to Jerusalem makes Jesus's allusion to Judges
19 more resonant for his own purposes.

35.   JSB 19.25n rightly notes that the "descriptions of time," the length of her
ordeal, "emphasizes the brutality."

36.   The Hebrew and most translations make it clear that he seeks to win
her back with kindness, from his heart; AV "speak friendly," RVS "speak
kindly," JSB "to woo her and win her back."

37.   For my using *wife* here see this chapter n. 33. I wish to avoid the English
connotations of concubine in this instance.

38.   *She* assembles the nation; he, for obvious reasons, must supply the
narrative, which he does in such a way as to rile everyone's blood and
exhort them to take revenge; see Judges 20.4–7.

39.   This would suggest Benjamin did not answer the initial summons, and
it might well be that the body part destined for them was ignored, if
sent to them at all. Twelve is something of a magic number here. The

Levite would not divide her into elevenths. It is the entire nation that
is disgraced unless it does something to avenge this outrage, so twelve
it must be. Perhaps the twelfth part of her stays with him, to keep him
on task.

40. The reformed churches, the Protestants, took it in varying degrees rather
more figuratively, for as John Wyclif, the proto-Protestant, writing in the
late fourteenth century would have it: "If thou [were to] see in liknesse
of fleisch and blood that blessed sacrament, thou schuldest lothen and
abhorren it to resseyve it into thy mouth," which is to say that if it really
were the body and blood, you would be disgusted, for that is what the
word *abhor* meant in fourteenth-century English; quoted in MED s.v.
abhorren. See p. 58.

41. Recall the homophone in English: host of the table and the sacrificial host
are not derived from the same root; see this chapter, n. 24.

42. *Hávamál*, st. 138.

43. A certain style of mystical devotion that focused its intensity on the
Eucharist used images of glutting, sating, and eating to describe taking in
the wafer. See Bynum, *Holy Feast and Holy Fast*; also her "Women Mystics
and Eucharistic Devotion."

44. See my "Choosing the Avenger," which deals with this bloody-token
ritual in detail.

45. In that instance in 1 Sam. 11 it is said that Saul's dismembered oxen work
not as a charge to take revenge but as a token of what he will do to those
who do not answer the summons to respond to Nahash the Ammonite's
offer to 'cut a covenant' by cutting out the right eye of the men of Jabesh
Gilead. 'To cut' is the literal meaning of the Hebrew verb used for
contracting, not unlike when we say 'to cut a deal.'

46. Note also that the last verse of the Book of Judges (21.25) reiterates the
first verse of Judges 19 that the times were kingless: and "every man did
that which was right in his own eyes." That is almost a refrain in Judges
17–21, a version of it mentioned four times. We can thus in part read
Jesus's recourse to the latter chapters of Judges using that refrain as a kind
of warrant for his renewing the kingship after its falling off from David
and Solomon.

47. Cf. OED s.v. remember, v.1, 5b.

Chapter 8

1. OED s.v. odds, n. 7a. 'odd ends' is first recorded 180 years earlier, s.v. odd,
adj., n. 1, and adv. 8a.

2. Compare late British English 'odds and sods' for pure rhyming attraction
with a more negative suggestion of the quality of the leftovers than is
borne by 'odds and ends.' As my friend and colleague John Hudson, an
Englishman, indicated to me in conversation, one could without shame
direct a guest to munch on the odds and ends in the fridge but not on

the odds and sods, which would be distinctly less inviting, which view is largely backed by the quoted passages in OED s.v. odds, n. 7b.

3. Old Norse has a similar idiom, *standask í odda*, to stand at odds, where the suggestion is that one party is seeking to get even with the other, but since the word *oddi* is related to *oddr*, that is, the point of a sword, knife, or spear, the metaphor is a bit richer in suggestiveness than English 'to be at odds' is. See, for example, Cleasby-Vigfusson, s.vv. oddi and oddr; see de Vries, 415.

4. The subject of the Quiggin Memorial Lecture, Cambridge University, I gave in December 2019, mostly on *Laxdæla saga*, ch. 75.

5. Austin, 4–11, passim.

6. LORD in all caps is how the King James Bible (AV) renders the tetragrammaton; 'Lord' in the AV renders Hebrew Adonai, the word for a human lord, which is said every time the tetragrammaton YHWH appears in the written text when it is read aloud (or silently). See also p. 96.

7. Lev. 24.15ff, but which text Philo extends to apply not only to overt blasphemous use of the NAME but also to any unauthorized use: "If any one, I do not say should blaspheme against the Lord of men and gods, but should even dare to utter his name unseasonably, let him expect the penalty of death." *Life of Moses* II.xxxviii (206).

8. Allen Sherman's send-up of it— "God bless ye Jerry Mandelbaum" in the medley "Shticks and Stones" (1962)—gave to Jews more punctilious than I a chance at least to sing the tune with kosher lyrics, while they could deny they were paying homage to the carol. https://www.youtube.com/watch?v=Cqz3NNQvBaI.

9. When I sent this to Nina for comments she emailed this: "For the record, definitely 'FD' provoked it. I do remember my discomfort at her bringing up her very sick grandmother. And while waiting in line for gym class!!" One sees that the battle to the death continues at least for one of the combatants, and despite the literature on the unreliability of childhood memory, this incident looks like Nina has it on film.

10. Bowen, 20.

11. Frost, "Design," vv. 11–14.

12. The thorn still lives in our world but fails to be recognized for what it is. It appears in kitsch names like Ye Olde Shoppe, the Y being not a Y but a deformed thorn, or simply how thorn came to be written in some Middle English and Scots hands, so it is in fact The Olde Shoppe. Also note that the *u* in *heuede* in the last line indicates a *v*.

13. One of the poems in the famed fourteenth-century Harley lyrics, named after the manuscript they are preserved in, MS Harley 2253, and reprinted in numerous anthologies. Facsimile here at f59v: http://www.bl.uk/manuscripts/Viewer.aspx?ref=harley_ms_2253_f001r.

14. Koestler, *Darkness at Noon*, 259 (in Kindle pagination). Cf. Steven Pinker writing from an upscale Boston suburb, and see my discussion (p. 37) of the pub game: "Worst century ever: does any beat the twentieth?"

15. See Katherine Mansfield's powerful "The Fly" (1923), which makes one care about a single fly being tormented, with no easy way to blame the tormentor.

16. It was surely better that I offered Hank Voltaire's aphorism than one confirming his discovery of the grand purposelessness of life from, say, Emil Cioran—"It is because it rests on nothing, because it lacks even the shadow of an argument that we persevere in life" (*A Short History of Decay*, 10). Cioran would be one of those journey-to-end-of-the-nighters Orwell would see fit to pillory; see pp. 98–99. That I actually subscribe to Voltaire's modestly practical counsel might be taken to show that my pessimism, while not completely a pretense, is not all that dark.

17. Tolkien's chilling concluding line of his famous essay: "*Beowulf*: The Monsters and the Critics."

Chapter 9

1. Freud deals with some of these in his short essay "The Antithetical Meaning of Primal Words."

2. It turns out that given the rate of insect die-off, this is less certain than I took it to be; cockroaches and humans might switch places in numerousness, as well as in spirit.

3. Charlotte Brontë, *Villette* (1853), ch. 11, which, as it happened, I was reading while writing the speech, has this: "It was his custom to mount straight to the nursery, taking about three degrees of the staircase at once."

4. The ease of going down can end up making it a welcome "all downhill from here," rather different in valence from being tossed down the stairs.

5. The law of future interests is a famous bugbear of the Anglo-American common law and the bane of every first-year Property student. I am tracking here the language of the notorious Rule against Perpetuities, much hated by students, for an explanation of which see my *Losing It*, 167–72.

WORKS CITED

300. Directed by Zack Snyder. Legendary Pictures. 2006.

Aeneid. See Virgil.

Aggesen. See Sven Aggesen.

Althoff, Gerd. *Family, Friends and Followers: Political and Social Bonds in Medieval Europe*. Translated by Christopher Carroll. Cambridge: Cambridge University Press, 2004.

Amarna Letters. [EA]. Translated and edited by William L. Moran. Baltimore: Johns Hopkins University Press, 1992.

Amira. See von Amira.

Anglo-Saxon Chronicle. MS E. http://asc.jebbo.co.uk/e/e-L.html. Translation at https://archive.org/stream/anglosaxonchroni00gile/anglosaxonchroni00gile_djvu.txt.

Anthony, St. *Athanasius of Alexandria: The Life of Antony: The Coptic Life and the Greek Life*. Translated by Tim Vivian. Kalamazoo, MI: Cistercian Publications, 2003.

Aquinas, St. Thomas. *Summa Theologiæ*. 1265–74. Blackfriars edition. New York: McGraw-Hill, 1964. http://www.newadvent.org/summa/index.html.

Aristotle. *Rhetoric*. Translated by W. Rhys Roberts. In *The Complete Works of Aristotle*. Edited by Jonathan Barnes. Princeton, NJ: Princeton University Press, 1984. Vol. 2: 2152–269.

Atkinson, James B., and David Sices, translators and editors. *Machiavelli and His Friends: Their Personal Correspondence*. DeKalb: Northern Illinois University Press, 1996.

Attenborough, F. L., editor and translator. *The Laws of the Earliest English Kings*. Cambridge: Cambridge University Press, 1922.

Augustine, St. *Confessions*. Edited and translated by Henry Chadwick. Oxford: Oxford University Press, 1991.

Austen, Jane. *Sense and Sensibility*. 1811. London: Penguin, 1995.

Austin, J. L. *How to Do Things with Words*. Cambridge, MA: Harvard University Press, 1962.

Bandamanna saga. Íslensk fornrit 7: 291–363. Edited by Guðni Jónsson. Reykjavík, 1936. Translated by Ruth C. Ellison as *The Saga of the Confederates*. In *Comic Sagas and Tales from Iceland*. Edited by Viðar Hreinsson. London: Penguin, 2013. 119–54.

Bao Ninh. *The Sorrow of War: A Novel of North Vietnam*. Translated by Phan Thanh Hao. New York: Pantheon, 1995.

Beowulf. Klaeber's Beowulf. 4th ed. Edited by R. D. Fulk, Robert E. Bjork, and John D. Niles. Toronto: University of Toronto Press, 2008.

Blok, Anton. "The Narcissism of Minor Differences." *European Journal of Social Theory* 1 (1998), 33–56.

Bosworth-Toller. *An Anglo-Saxon Dictionary*; based on the manuscript collections of Joseph Bosworth. Supplement by T. Northcote Toller. Oxford: Clarendon, 1972. http://www.bosworthtoller.com/.

Bowen, Elizabeth. *The House in Paris*. 1935. New York: Knopf, 1936.

Brontë, Charlotte. *Villette*. 1853. Oxford: Oxford World Classics reissue, 2000. Kindle version.

Browne, Sir Thomas. *Religio Medici*. 1643. In *Religio Medici and Hydriotaphia, or Urne-Buriall*. Edited with introduction by Stephen Greenblatt and Ramie Targoff. New York: New York Review of Books, 2012.

Bynum, Caroline Walker. *Holy Feast and Holy Fast: The Religious Significance of Food to Medieval Women*. Berkeley: University of California Press, 1987.

Bynum, Caroline Walker. "Women Mystics and Eucharistic Devotion in the Thirteenth Century." In her *Fragmentation and Redemption: Essays on Gender and the Human Body in Medieval Religion*. New York: Zone Books, 1992.

Caesar. Vol. III. *Alexandrian War, African War, Spanish War*. Translated by A. G. Way. Loeb Classical Library, 401. Cambridge, MA: Harvard University Press, 1955.

Catholic Encyclopedia. 1907–12. https://www.catholic.org/encyclopedia/.

Chaucer, Geoffrey. "The Merchant's Tale." In *The Works of Geoffrey Chaucer*. Edited by F. N. Robinson. Boston: Houghton Mifflin, 1957. https://quod.lib.umich.edu/c/cme/CT/1:4.4?rgn=div2;view=fulltext.

Cioran, E. M. *A Short History of Decay*. 1949. Translated by Richard Howard, 1975. New York: Arcade Publishing, 2012.

Cleasby-Vigfusson. *An Icelandic-English Dictionary*. Edited by Richard Cleasby and Gudbrand Vigfusson. 2nd ed. by Sir William A. Craigie. Oxford: Clarendon, 1957. https://www.ling.upenn.edu/~kurisuto/germanic/oi_cleasbyvigfusson_about.html.

Cuddihy, John Murray. The *Ordeal of Civility: Freud, Marx, Lévi-Strauss, and the Jewish Struggle with Modernity*. New York: Basic Books, 1974.

Curtis, Valerie et al. "Disgust as an Adaptive System for Disease Avoidance Behaviour." *Philosophical Transactions of the Royal Society of London. Series B, Biological Sciences* 366, no. 1563 (2011), 389–401. https://www.ncbi.nlm.nih.gov/pmc/articles/PMC3013466/.

de Vries, Jan. *Altnordisches Etymologisches Wörterbuch*. 2nd ed. Leiden: Brill, 1962.

DeWitte, Sharon N. "Stress, Sex, and Plague: Patterns of Developmental Stress and Survival in Pre- and Post-Black Death London." *American Journal of Human Biology* 30 (2018), e23073.

Dickens, Charles. *Our Mutual Friend*. 1865. http://www.gutenberg.org/ebooks/883.

EA. See *Amarna Letters*.

Edwards, Peter. "Honour, Shame, Humiliation and Modern Japan." In *Friendship East and West: Philosophical Perspectives*. Edited by Oliver Leaman. Surrey: Curzon, 1996. 32–155.

Eclogues. See Virgil.

Egils saga. *Egils saga Skalla-Grímssonar*. Edited by Sigurður Nordal. Íslenzk fornrit 2. Reykjavík, 1933. Translated by Richard Scudder. *Egil's Saga*. London: Penguin, 2002.

Elster, Jon. *Nuts and Bolts for the Social Sciences*. Cambridge: Cambridge University Press, 1989.

Eyrbyggja saga. Íslenzk fornrit 4: 1–184. Edited by Einar Ól. Sveinsson and Matthías Þórðarson. Reykjavík, 1935. Translated by Hermann Pálsson and Paul Edwards. Harmondsworth: Penguin, 1989.

Faraone, Christopher A. "Molten Wax, Spilt Wine and Mutilated Animals: Sympathetic Magic in Near Eastern and Early Greek Oath Ceremonies." *Journal of Hellenic Studies* 113 (1993), 60–80.

Franklin, Benjamin. *Autobiography, Poor Richard and Later Writing*. Edited by J. A. Leo Lemay. New York: Library of America, 1997. 565–729.

Freud, Sigmund. "The Antithetical Meaning of Primal Words." 1911. In *The Standard Edition of the Complete Psychological Works of Sigmund Freud*. Edited by James Strachey. London: Hogarth Press, 1953–1974. 24 vols. 11.155–61.

Freud, Sigmund. *Jokes and Their Relation to the Unconscious*. 1905. In *The Standard Edition of the Complete Psychological Works of Sigmund Freud*. Edited by James Strachey. London: Hogarth Press, 1953–1974. 24 vols. Vol. 8.

Freud, Sigmund. *Three Essays on the Theory of Sexuality*. 1901–5. In *The Standard Edition of the Complete Psychological Works of Sigmund Freud*. Edited by James Strachey. London: Hogarth Press, 1953–1974. 24 vols. 7.125–323.

Frost, Robert. *The Poetry of Robert Frost: The Collected Poems, Prose, and Plays*. Edited by R. Poirier and M. Richardson. New York: Library of America, 1995.

Gade, Kari Ellen. "'1236: Oprækja meiddr ok heill görr.'" *Gripla* 9 (1995), 115–32.

Gerald of Wales. (Geraldus Cambrensis). *Gemma Ecclesiastica*. Edited by J. S. Brewer. Opera 2. Rerum Britannicarum Medii Aevi Scriptores (Rolls Series), vol. 21. London, 1862. Translation by John J. Hagen. Davis Medieval Texts and Studies, vol. 2. Leiden: Brill, 1979.

Gluckman, Max. "Moral Crises: Magical and Secular Solutions." In *The Allocation of Responsibility*. Edited by Max Gluckman. Manchester: Manchester University Press, 1972. 1–50.

Goffman, Erving. *The Presentation of Self in Everyday Life*. New York: Anchor, 1959.

Goffman, Erving. *Relations in Public*. New York: Basic Books, 1971.

Grágás: Islændernes Lovbog i fristatens Tid. 3 vols. Edited by Vilhjálmur Finsen. 1852 (Konungsbók), 1879 (Staðarhólsbók), 1883. Copenhagen. Rpt. Odense, 1974. Translation of Konungsbók with selections from Staðarhólsbók and other mss: *Laws of Early Iceland: Grágás. The Codex Regius of Grágás with Material from Other Manuscripts*. 2 vols. 1980, 2000. Translated by Andrew Dennis, Peter Foote, and Richard Perkins. Winnipeg: University of Manitoba Press. Vol. 1 contains *Grágás* Ia 1-Ia 217; vol. 2, *Grágás* Ia 218-Ib 218 in Finsen's pagination.

Grammaticus. See Saxo.

Green, D. H. *Language and History in the Early Germanic World*. Cambridge: Cambridge University Press, 1998.

Gregory of Tours (d. 594 CE). *The History of the Franks*. Translated by Lewis Thorpe. Harmondsworth: Penguin, 1974.

Groebner, Valentin. *Liquid Assets, Dangerous Gifts: Presents and Politics at the End of the Middle Ages*. Translated by Pamela E. Selwyn. Philadelphia: University of Pennsylvania Press, 2002.

Grønbech, Vilhelm. *The Culture of the Teutons*. 1909–12. Translated by W. Worseter. London: Humphrey Milford, Oxford University Press, 1931. https://archive.org/stream/VilhelmGrnbechCultureOfTheTeutons/Vilhelm%20Gr%C3%B6nbech%20-%20Culture%20of%20the%20Teutons_djvu.txt.

Guðmundar saga dýra. In *Sturlunga saga* 1: 160–212. Translated at 2: 145–206.

Hamlet. See Shakespeare, William.

Harley Lyrics. The Harley Lyrics: The Middle English Lyrics of MS. Harley 2253. Edited by G. L. Brook. Manchester: University of Manchester Press, 1956. https://quod.lib.umich.edu/c/cme/HarLyr?rgn=main;view=fulltext.

Hartley, L. P. *The Go-Between*. 1953. New York: New York Review of Books, 2002.

Hávamál. In *Edda: die Lieder des Codex Regius*. 3rd ed. Edited by Hans Kuhn. Heidelberg: Carl Winter, 1962. 17–44. Translated by Patricia Terry, *Poems of the Vikings: The Elder Edda*. Indianapolis: Bobbs-Merrill, 1969. More recently: *The Cowboy Hávamál*, by Jackson Crawford also in his *The Poetic Edda: Stories of the Norse Gods and Heroes*. Indianapolis: Hackett, 2015. 341–52. https://jacksonwcrawford.com/the-cowboy-havamal/.

Herodotus: The Histories. Translated by Tom Holland. Introduction and notes by Paul Cartledge. London: Penguin, 2013.

Historia Augusta. Vol. 1: *Life of Septimius Severus*. Translated by David Magie. Loeb Classical Library, 139. Cambridge, MA: Harvard University Press, 1921. 371–430. http://penelope.uchicago.edu/Thayer/E/Roman/Texts/Historia_Augusta/Septimius_Severus*.html.

Hittite Diplomatic Texts. 2nd ed. Translated by Gary Beckman. Society of Biblical Literature: Writings from the Ancient World, Series 7. Atlanta: Scholars Press, 1999.

Hobbes, Thomas. *The Elements of Law, Natural and Politic: Part I: Human Nature; Part II: De Corpore Politico with Three Lives*. 1640. Edited by J. C. A. Gaskin. Oxford: Oxford University Press, 1994.

Hobbes, Thomas. *Leviathan*. 1651. Edited by E. M. Curley. Indianapolis: Hackett 1994.

Homer. See *Iliad*.

Hrafnkel's saga. Hrafnkels saga Freysgoða. Edited by Jón Jóhannesson. Íslenzk fornrit 11.95–133. Reykjavík, 1950. Translated by Hermann Pálsson. In *Hrafnkel's Saga and Other Stories*, 35–71. Harmondsworth: Penguin, 1971, also by Miller, *Hrafnkel or the Ambiguities*, 217–34.

Hrólfs saga kraka. In *Fornaldar Sögur Norðurlanda*, vol. 1. Edited by Guðni Jónsson. Reykjavík: Íslendingasagnaútgáfan, 1954. Translated by Jesse Byock. *The Saga of King Hrolf Kraki*. London: Penguin, 1998.

Iliad. Homer. 2nd ed. Revised by William F. Wyatt. Loeb Classical Library, 170–71. Cambridge, MA: Harvard University Press, 1999.

Íslendinga saga. In *Sturlunga saga* 1: 229–608. Translated at 1: 115–447.

Jewish Study Bible. Edited by Adele Berlin and Marc Zvi Brettler. Oxford, 2004.

JSB. See *Jewish Study Bible*.

Ker, W. P. *Epic and Romance: Essays on Medieval Literature*. 1897. New York: Dover Publications, 1957.

Kilger, Christoph. "Wholeness and Holiness: Counting, Weighing and Valuing Silver in the Early Viking Period." In *Means of Exchange: Dealing with Silver in the Viking Age*. Edited by Dagfinn Skre. Kaupang Excavation Project Publication Series, vol. 2. Aarhus: Aarhus University Press, 2008. 253–325.

King Lear. See Shakespeare, William.

Koestler, Arthur. *Darkness at Noon*. Translated by Daphne Hardy. New York: Macmillan, 1941. Kindle edition: Simon and Schuster, 2019.

Koziol, Geoffrey. *Begging Pardon and Favor: Ritual and Political Order in Early Medieval France*. Ithaca, NY: Cornell University Press, 1992.

La Rochefoucauld, *Maxims*. 1665, 1st ed. Translated by Leonard Tancock. Harmondsworth: Penguin, 1959.

Lawing, Sean B. *Perspectives on Disfigurement in Medieval Iceland: A Cultural Study Based on Old Norse Laws and Icelandic Sagas*. PhD diss. University of Iceland. Reykjavík: Háskólaprent, 2016.

Laxdæla saga. Edited by Einar Ól. Sveinsson. Íslenzk fornrit 5. Reykjavík, 1934. Translated by Magnus Magnusson and Hermann Pálsson. Harmondsworth: Penguin, 1969.

Letter from Šulgi to Aradĝu about Apillaša. ETCSL Project. Oriental Studies, Oxford University, 2006. http://etcsl.orinst.ox.ac.uk/cgi-bin/etcsl. cgi?text=t.3.1.02#.

Lewis, Sinclair. *Babbitt*. New York: Harcourt, Brace, 1922. http://www. gutenberg.org/files/1156/1156-h/1156-h.htm.

Lichtheim, Miriam. *Ancient Egyptian Literature:* vol. 2. *The New Kingdom.* 1973. Berkeley: University of California Press, 2006.

Liebermann, Felix. *Die Gesetze der Angelsachsen.* 3 vols. Halle: Niemeyer, 1903–16.

Ljósvetninga saga. Edited by Björn Sigfússon. Íslenzk fornrit 10:1–139. Reykjavík, 1940. Translated by Theodore M. Anderson and William Ian Miller. In *Law and Literature in Medieval Iceland.* Stanford: Stanford University Press, 1989. 119–255.

Machiavelli, Niccolò. *The Prince.* 1513. Translated and edited by Robert M. Adams. 2nd ed. New York: Norton, 1992. https://www.earlymoderntexts. com/assets/pdfs/machiavelli1532.pdf.

Machiavelli, Niccolò. For his correspondence, see under Atkinson, James B., and David Sices.

MacLean, Simon, translator and annotator. *History and Politics in Late Carolingian and Ottonian Europe: The Chronicle of Regino of Prüm and Adalbert of Magdeburg.* Manchester: Manchester University Press, 2009.

Mansfield, Katherine. "The Fly." 1923. In *Stories.* New York: Vintage, 1991.

Mark VII. (pseudonym of Max Plowman). *A Subaltern on the Somme in 1916.* New York: Dutton, 1928.

Martín-Durán, José M. et al. "The Developmental Basis for the Recurrent Evolution of Deuterostomy and Protostomy." *Nature, Ecology & Evolution* 1 (2016). Article number: 0005 (2016). https://www.nature.com/articles/ s41559-016-0005#supplementary-information.

Mauss, Marcel. *The Gift.* Original: *Essai sur le don: forme et raison de l'échange dans les sociétés archaïques,* 1923–24. Translated by W. D. Halls. Introduction by Mary Douglas. New York: Routledge, 1990.

McDonagh, Martin. See *Seven Psychopaths.*

McDonough, James. *Platoon Leader.* Novato, CA: Presidio, 1985.

MED. See *Middle English Dictionary.*

Meier, Samuel A. *The Messenger in the Ancient Semitic World.* Harvard Semitic Monographs 45. Atlanta: Scholars Press, 1989.

Michalowski, Piotr. *Letters from Early Mesopotamia.* Atlanta: Scholars Press, 1993.

Middle English Dictionary. Edited by Hans Kurath. Ann Arbor: University of Michigan Press, 1952–2001. https://quod.lib.umich.edu/m/ middle-english-dictionary.

Miller, William Ian. *The Anatomy of Disgust.* Cambridge, MA: Harvard University Press, 1997.

Miller, William Ian. *Audun and the Polar Bear: Luck, Law, and Largesse in a Medieval Tale of Risky Business.* Leiden: Brill, 2008.

Miller, William Ian. "Choosing the Avenger: Some Aspects of the Bloodfeud in Medieval Iceland and England." *Law and History Review* 1 (1983), 159–204.

Miller, William Ian. "Deep Inner Lives, Individualism, and People of Honour." *History of Political Thought* 16 (1995), 190–207.

Miller, William Ian. "Dégoût." In *Passions sociales*. Edited by Gloria Origgi. Paris: Presses Universitaires de France, 2019. 162–68.

Miller, William Ian. "Epilogue: Do I Disgust You? (Or Rather, You Me?) mes frères, mes sœurs, mes semblables?" In *Le Dégoût: Histoire, langage, esthétique et politique*. Edited by Michel Delville, Andrew Norris, and Viktoria von Hoffmann. Liège: Presses Universitaires de Liège, 2015. 149–61.

Miller, William Ian. *Eye for an Eye*. Cambridge: Cambridge University Press, 2006.

Miller, William Ian. *Faking It*. Cambridge: Cambridge University Press, 2003.

Miller, William Ian. *Hrafnkel or the Ambiguities: Hard Cases, Hard Choices*. Oxford: Oxford University Press, 2017.

Miller, William Ian. *Humiliation: And Other Essays on Honor, Social Discomfort, and Violence*. Ithaca, NY: Cornell University Press, 1993.

Miller, William Ian. *Losing It, in which an aging professor laments his shrinking brain, which he flatters himself formerly did him noble service: A plaint, tragic-comical, historical, vengeful, sometimes satirical and thankful in six parts, if his memory does yet serve*. New Haven: Yale University Press, 2011.

Miller, William Ian. *"May You Have My Luck." The Chronicle Review* in *The Chronicle of Higher Education*, Feb. 6, 2015.

Miller, William Ian. "The Messenger." In *Frieden stiften: Vermittlung und Konfliktslösung vom Mittelalter bis heute*. Edited by Gerd Althoff. Darmstadt: *WBG*, 2011. 19–36.

Miller, William Ian. *The Mystery of Courage*. Cambridge, MA: Harvard University Press, 2000.

Miller, William Ian. "Threat." In *Feud, Violence and Practice: Essays in Medieval Studies in Honor of Stephen D. White*. Edited by Belle S. Tuten and Tracey L. Billado. Farnham, Surrey: Ashgate, 2010. 9–28.

Miller, William Ian. *"Why Is Your Axe Bloody?": A Reading of Njáls Saga*. Oxford: Oxford University Press, 2014.

Milton, John. *Paradise Lost*. 1667. Edited by Gordon Teskey. New York: Norton, 2005.

Montaigne (d. 1592). *Michel de Montaigne: The Complete Essays*. Translated by M. A. Screech. Harmondsworth: Penguin, 1991.

Montecuccoli, Raimondo. (d. 1680). *Sulle battaglie*. Edited and translated by Thomas M. Barker. In *The Military Intellectual and Battle: Raimondo Montecuccoli and the Thirty Years War*. Albany: SUNY Press, 1975.

NGL. *Norges gamle Love indtil 1387*. 1846. Vol. 1. Edited by R. Keyser and P. A. Munch. Christiania [Oslo]. Most of volume 1 translated by Laurence M. Larson. *The Earliest Norwegian Laws, Being the Gulathing Law and the Frostathing Law*. New York: Columbia University Press, 1935.

Nietzsche, Friedrich. *On the Genealogy of Morals*. 1887. Translated by Walter Kaufmann and R. J. Hollingdale. New York: Vintage, 1967.

Njal's saga. Brennu-Njáls saga. Edited by Einar Ól. Sveinsson. Íslenzk fornrit 12. Reykjavík, 1954. Translated by Magnus Magnusson and Hermann Pálsson. Baltimore: Penguin, 1960.

O'Brien, Bruce R. *God's Peace and King's Peace: The Laws of Edward the Confessor.* Philadelphia: University of Pennsylvania Press, 1999.

OED. *Oxford English Dictionary.* 3rd ed. Oxford: Oxford University Press, 2005. http://www.oed.com/.

Orwell, George. "Inside the Whale." 1940. In *George Orwell: The Collected Essays, Journalism, and Letters.* Vol. 1: *An Age Like This: 1920–1940.* Edited by Sonia Orwell and Ian Angus. New York: Harcourt Brace, 1968. 493–527.

Pactus Legis Salicae. Edited by Karl August Eckhardt. Göttingen: Musterschmidt, 1955. Translated by Katherine Fisher Drew, *The Laws of the Salian Franks.* Philadelphia: University of Pennsylvania Press, 1991.

Parkinson, R. B., translator and editor. *The Tale of Sinuhe and Other Ancient Egyptian Poems, 1940–1640 BC.* Oxford: Oxford University Press, 1997.

Payer, Pierre J. *The Bridling of Desire: Views of Sex in the Later Middle Ages.* Toronto: University of Toronto Press, 1993.

Pepys. *The Diary of Samuel Pepys.* 11 vols. Edited by Robert Latham and William Matthes. Berkeley: University of California Press, 2000.

Philo. *Life of Moses.* In *Philo,* vol. VI. Loeb Classical Library, 289. Cambridge, MA: Harvard University Press, 1984.

Pinker, Steven. *The Better Angels of Our Nature: Why Violence Has Declined.* New York: Viking, 2011.

Pokorny, Julius. *Indogermanisches Etymologisches Wörterbuch.* 4th ed. Tübingen: A. Francke, 2002.

Rezzori, Gregor von. See von Rezzori.

Royal Frankish Annals. In *Carolingian Chronicles.* Translated by Bernhard Walter Scholz. Ann Arbor: University of Michigan Press, 1970. 35–127. https://babel.hathitrust.org/cgi/pt?id=mdp.39015015186805;view=1up;seq=8.

Rozin, Paul, and April E. Fallon. "A Perspective on Disgust." *Psychological Review* 94 (1987), 23–41.

Saxo Grammaticus. *Gesta Danorum: The History of the Danes.* 2 vols. Edited by Karsten Friis-Jensen. Translated by Peter Fisher. Oxford: Clarendon Press, 2015.

Seven Psychopaths. Directed by Martin McDonagh. Blueprint Pictures. 2012.

Shakespeare, William. *As You Like It.* Edited by Juliet Dusinberre. The Arden Shakespeare. London: Thomson Learning, 2006.

Shakespeare, William. *Hamlet.* Edited by Harold Jenkins. The Arden Shakespeare. New York: Methuen, 1982.

Shakespeare, William. *King Lear.* Edited by R. A. Foakes. The Arden Shakespeare. London: Thomas Nelson, 1997.

Shakespeare, William. *The Merchant of Venice.* Edited by John Russell Brown. The Arden Shakespeare. New York: Methuen, 1955.

Shakespeare, William. *Twelfth Night.* Edited by Keir Elam. The Arden Shakespeare. London: Cengage Learning, 2007.

Shapiro, James. *Shakespeare and the Jews.* New York: Columbia University Press, 1996.

Sherman, Allen. *My Son the Folk Singer*. Warner Brothers, 1962.

Shklar, Judith. *Ordinary Vices*. Cambridge, MA: Harvard University Press, 1984.

Simmel, Georg. (d. 1918). *The Sociology of Georg Simmel*. Translated and edited by Kurt H. Wolff. New York: Free Press, 1950. https://archive.org/stream/ sociologyofgeorg030082mbp/sociologyofgeorg030082mbp_djvu.txt.

Smith, Adam. *The Theory of Moral Sentiments*. Edited by D. D. Raphael and A. L. Macfie. 1759, 1st ed. Oxford: Clarendon, 1976.

Snorri Sturluson (d. 1241). *Edda: Prologue and Gylfaginning*. Edited by Anthony Faulkes. 2nd ed. Viking Society for Northern Research: University College London, 2005. http://www.vsnrweb-publications.org.uk/Edda-1.pdf. Translation: Faulkes. *Snorri Sturluson: Edda*. London: Dent, 1987.

Southern, R. W. "Aspects of the European Tradition of Historical Writing: 3. History as Prophecy." *Transactions of the Royal Historical Society* 22 (1972), 159–80. Repr. in *History and Historians: Selected Papers of R. W. Southern*. Edited by Robert Bartlett. Malden, MA: Blackwell, 2004. 48–65.

Stendhal. *The Scarlet and Black*. 1830. Translated by Margaret R. B. Shaw. Harmondsworth: Penguin, 1953.

Strickland, Matthew. *War and Chivalry: The Conduct and Perception of War in England and Normandy, 1066–1217*. Cambridge: Cambridge University Press, 1996.

Sturlunga saga. Edited by Jón Jóhannesson, Magnús Finnbogason, and Kristján Eldjárn. 2 vols. Sturlunguútgáfan: Reykjavík, 1946. Translated by Julia H. McGrew and R. George Thomas. 2 vols. New York: Twayne, 1970–74.

Sturlu saga. In *Sturlunga saga* 1: 63–114. Translated at 1: 59–113.

Suetonius. *The Twelve Caesars*. Translated by Robert Graves. Harmondsworth: Penguin, 1957.

Sven Aggesen. *The Works of Sven Aggesen Twelfth-Century Danish Historian*. Translated with introduction and notes by Eric Christiansen. Viking Society for Northern Research: University College London, 1992. *Lex Castrensis*, 31– 47. http://www.vsnrweb-publications.org.uk/Text%20Series/Sven.pdf.

Swift, Jonathan. "Verses on the Death of Dr. Swift." Written 1731, published 1739. Edited by Jack Lynch. https://andromeda.rutgers.edu/~jlynch/Texts/ verses.html.

Tacitus, Cornelius. *The Annals*. Translated by Alfred John Church and William Jackson Brodribb. 1876. Reprinted as part of *The Complete Works of Tacitus*. New York: Random House, 1942. Reprinted as *The Annals*. Edited by Sara Bryant for the Perseus Project, 2011. http://www.perseus.tufts.edu/hopper/text ?doc=Perseus%3Atext%3A1999.02.0078%3Abook%3D15%3Achapter%3D67.

Tacitus, Cornelius. *The History*. Ibid. http://www.perseus.tufts.edu/hopper/text? doc=Perseus%3Atext%3A1999.02.0080%3Abook%3D1%3Achapter%3D1.

Tolkien, J. R. R. "*Beowulf:* The Monsters and the Critics." *Proceedings of the British Academy* 22 (1936), 245–95.

Virgil (Vergil). *Aeneid*. Edited by J. B. Greenough. Boston: Ginn, 1897. http:// www.perseus.tufts.edu/hopper/text?doc=Perseus:text:1999.02.0055.

Virgil. *Eclogues*. Edited by J. B. Greenough. Boston: Ginn, 1900. http://www.
    perseus.tufts.edu/hopper/text?doc=Perseus%3Atext%3A1999.02.0056%3Apoe
    m%3D8.

Vlastos, Gregory. "Equality and Justice in Early Greek Cosmologies." *Classical
    Philology* 42 (1947), 156–78. http://www.jstor.org.proxy.lib.umich.edu/stable/
    265987.

Voltaire. *Dictionnaire Philosophique*. In *Œuvres complètes*, vols. 17–20.
    Paris: Garnier, 1878. Online entry for letter N: https://fr.wikisource.org/wiki/
    Dictionnaire_philosophique/Garnier_(1878)/Index_alphab%C3%A9tique/N.

von Amira, Karl. *Nordgermanisches Obligationenrecht*. Vol. 2: *Westnordisches
    Obligationenrecht*. Leipzig: von Veit, 1895.

von Rezzori, Gregor. *Memoirs of an Anti-Semite*. 1969. Translated in part by the
    author and part by Joachim Neugroschel. New York: Vintage, 1991.

Wolff, Tobias. *In Pharaoh's Army: Memories of the Lost War*.
    New York: Vintage, 1994.

Wrangham, Richard. *The Goodness Paradox: The Strange Relationship between
    Virtue and Violence in Human Evolution*. New York: Pantheon, 2019.

Zelizer, Viviana A. *Pricing the Priceless Child: The Changing Social Value of
    Children*. 1985. With new preface: Princeton, NJ: Princeton University
    Press, 1994.

Þorgils saga ok Hafliða. In *Sturlunga saga* 1: 12–50. Translated at 2: 25–70.

Þorgils saga skarða. In *Sturlunga saga* 2: 104–226. Translated at 2: 345–485.

INDEX